A
(

science and the manager

science and the manager

R. W. REVANS
Professor of Industrial Administration
The Manchester College of Science and
Technology

MACDONALD: LONDON

First Published in 1965 by
Macdonald & Co. (Publishers) Ltd.
Gulf House, 2 Portman Street, London W.1.
Made and Printed in the Republic of Ireland by Hely Thom Limited, Dublin

CONTENTS

ACKNOWLEDGEMENTS

The author and publisher wish to express their thanks to the Editors of the following journals for permission to reprint the articles mentioned:

Management International for *Science and the Manager;* Researches and Studies (University of Leeds Institute of Education) for *A Study of Technical Knowledge* and *Industrial Relations and Industrial Training;* Advanced Management Journal for *The Pathology of Automation* (this article has also appeared in Scientific Management); The Accountants' Magazine for *The Scope of Management Control.*

PREFACE

It was once held to be a mark of breeding among Cambridge men that they should apologise for their books, and among Oxford men that they should refrain from writing any. But another book about management demands more than an apology; one has a public duty to explain it. For the time of Britain's managers is one of her most precious assets, and none, by distracting their attention, should deliberately multiply the opportunities for its misuse. The suggestion that these papers should be published came originally from my wife; she felt that, if the real nature of their contents were more widely known, this might help to reduce the number of calls upon me to appear at conferences, so sparing her a scheduling task both irksome and unrewarded. This disclosure of its origins, if not lost upon the wives of certain other speakers, might well prove the greatest merit that the work possesses.

This is, therefore, no treatise on management; it is a collection of essays, written over the past twenty years. Some were suggested as addresses to conferences, others as memoranda intended to influence committees; a few were written for technical journals. But, as a prudent street-trader sorts through yesterday's left-over tomatoes before offering them for sale today, so have I attempted to remove from yesterday's thoughts those misconceptions so gross that my audiences have occasionally identified them with the so-called principles of management. If I tend to illustrate some common theme it is because, first, there is a need for applying the methods and attitudes of experimental science to the practice of industrialists; second, that when this is done there remain a number of exceedingly difficult problems requiring more than any known scientific method to solve them; and third, that the study of management and the development of theory from such study are still most rudimentary. If they are to advance, a great deal of research, far beyond any yet contemplated, will be needed. Some brief indication of what, in my opinion, is needed, should be visible in these papers.

The life of the individual is, alas, so complex and the lives of different individuals so varied that general pronouncements upon how even to identify their problems of decision seem premature. We need more research into what managers actually do and into what results, if any, these actions produce. Our progress in this is not helped much (if it is helped at all) by preferring to study branches of general knowledge germane to management rather than the specific activities of managers at first hand; and I feel that much of the indifference of industrialists to management education reflects their belief that the universities cannot deal their essential management problems anything more than a glancing blow. Even less charitably put, the professor cannot bridge the chasm between the factory and the university merely by shooting it full of academic hardcore chipped out here and there from the pages of his existing university calendar. This criticism must be acknowledged as half true; we do not know enough to display a map of the world of management in the way that, for example, Hegel tried to display a map of history or Kant a map of truth; we still await our Mathew Paris. It may well be that such a map is impossible to draw, and that one day we shall abandon the search for it, as, around the middle of the seventeenth century, the realists gave up their attempts to draw the map of Heaven.

The truths of management may well never form a seamless garment; and we, the teachers, may be forever forced, in maintaining our disguise of scholarship, to dress in second-hand suits. But there remains plenty to think about; perhaps we can set out, for example, to define what is meant by "expanding production" and to determine whether British industry is or is not, on average, achieving it; we could then ask whether the expansion, if any, depends at all upon the activities of our managers and, if so, to what degree and why. We could enquire in what circumstances these managers could be expected to do anything different, or even, perhaps, something better. These empirical exercises all seem to me important, interesting and difficult. And when we have done them we can then, perhaps, sit down to our comprehensive treatise on management, and our universal syllabus for the education of those who practise it. In the meantime I find it arduous enough to string together even the simplest managerial ideas.

Of the matters dealt with in these papers, I hope in the near future to treat at greater length in forthcoming books on SAMPLING OF SHOP FLOOR ATTITUDES and DECIS-ION MAKING. The present volume is to be followed by a second volume of collected papers around the theme of management education.

THE SAMPLING OF
SHOP FLOOR ATTITUDES

1. The Analysis of Managerial Relations

The future of management as a teachable subject, in the sense that, say, dentistry is considered to be a teachable subject, depends upon our progress in understanding the relations of the manager to those with whom he works. This understanding, moreover, must allow us to describe these relations in terms of the observable activities of the management situation; it is inadequate to "explain" them in terms of innate or subjective qualities, such as flair, leadership or hunch. No doubt, at the present level of our understanding we admit that some managers are better at hunching than are others. But if we are to set ourselves up as management analysts, and as management teachers, we must examine these observable differences in the hope that they can be attributed to causes over which it is possible to exercise some deliberate control. We are, in the 1960's, in much the same situation as was French brewing a century ago, when Louis Pasteur was demonstrating that the beer was turned sour not by causes spontaneously generated in particular vats, but by subtle and invisible influences insinuating themselves in from outside. We cannot hope, in the field of management, to discriminate between the spontaneous generation of destructive

2

influences within the manager himself, on the one hand, and the invasion of his field by external corruption, on the other, until we have studied more deeply the precise nature of his relations with what is going on around him. Such study demands a methodology no less to be subjected to analysis and test than have the methodologies of physics or of engineering, where theory and practice have not only survived but have been nourished by the criticism of several centuries.

The concepts of analysis and of test demand that there is a structure to be analysed and a set of propositions to be tested. We cannot, in discussing the relations of a manager to those around him, usefully suggest from first principles or by elaborate ratiocination what this structure and these propositions should be, although we may speculate upon them. Our first need is to collect evidence; our second need is to put this evidence into order; our third need is to demonstrate that this order differs significantly from one management situation to another; and our fourth is to show that these significant differences are associated with factors of the situations over which the management might, given ingenuity enough, exercise conscious influence. We may illustrate this by reference to recent work upon the management of hospitals. Evidence here showed that comparable groups of patients in different hospitals recovered at markedly different average rates, or, at least, were discharged after markedly different average lengths of stay. If these differences were in any way to be ascribed to differences in management relations, what were the structures of these relations, and how could they be consciously modified? Firstly, what evidence should be collected? Secondly, into what order is this evidence to be put? Thirdly, can it be demonstrated that this order differs significantly between the different hospitals? Fourthly, are these significant differences associated with factors within the hospitals over which their managements can learn to exercise deliberate control?

A set of answers to these questions has been found; it is probable that other sets are no less valid, since there may, in reality, be many causes helping to determine that the average length of stay of, say adult male appendicectomies in one hospital is greater than the average in another. Nevertheless, it is always helpful to identify at least one set of causes; we must not complain when, in using a new method to attack a problem, our victory is not entirely complete. In the present example, the answers to our four questions are as follow: firstly, we collect evidence about the ward sister's ability to communicate with her superiors and with her subordinates; secondly, we choose, from the evidence so collected, a scheme of classification that enables us to assign numerical values to certain aspects of the sister's ability to communicate; thirdly, we demonstrate that, with the numerical values so assigned, there are highly significant differences between the communication systems of the various hospitals examined; fourthly, we further demonstrate that these significant differences are both statistically associated with the different averages of patient stay, and that they could, in all probability, be consciously amended by those in charge of the hospital. We need to extend this kind of examination to the communication networks of industry and commerce, bearing in mind, of course, the great economic and political differences between hospitals, on the one hand, and business, on the other.

2. A Study of Attitudes to Change

A small contribution to the development of this corner of management methodology has recently been made through a study of the attitudes of Lancashire factory workers towards change. It is an opinion frequently expressed by managers in the north of England that their employees will always resist innovation on its own account, and certainly the history of the textile industry lends support to this pessimistic thesis. It is not entirely fanciful to suggest that the drift of population to the south of England is encouraged by the hopes of managers to find a less inflexible labour force. But a preliminary study of the difficulties encountered over the introduction of Work Study, itself the messenger of innovation, suggested a somewhat different explanation: that the Lancashire workman was not hostile to innovation as such but rather that he tended to mistrust it, in some factories, because it was advocated by a management in whom he had no confidence.

It may well be the economic policy of a board of directors to increase the output of their enterprise (and the wages of their employees) by introducing new methods of work, or new designs, or different raw materials, or more efficient plant, but it is of no use their reckoning without the response of the workpeople upon whose efforts this policy of enhanced productivity must eventually depend. Whatever their economic intentions, they must be fully seized of the managerial problem, and if they believe that resistance to change, like beer going sour, is spontaneously generated among their labour force rather than introduced into the factory situation by their own unpopularity, then the future of their innovating policy is likely to be one of discord and failure. One cannot control any situation that one does not understand, and among the most uncontrollable situations of all are those in which the two parties to a contract each wrongly impute the difficulties of implementing it to the other. In the example here given, the workpeople may grossly misinterpret the present motives of their managers, and these in turn are completely unaware that those on the shop floor might, in fact, be perfectly willing to support any change whatever if they could be convinced that it was not entirely a piece of exploitation by their own ambiguously-motivated management. Nowhere can the meaning of satisfactory communications be more clearly illustrated than in such common examples as these; nowhere is the distinction between sound economic goals and inefficient managerial actions more sharply contrasted.

3. An Excursion into Measurement

Consider, then, the following three statements:
> "So long as you get your fair day's work done, the foreman does not bother you."

"When anybody slacks, the rest suffer for it in the long run."

"Here we work with the management as a team."

These, with many hundreds of others, were recorded in the course of a study, extending over several years, of the attitudes of Lancashire workers to life in the factory, with especial attention to their attitudes to innovation. The research worker was a Pakistani, a young graduate mechanical engineer; it is likely that the many hundreds of factory workers whom he interviewed spoke to him with a freedom that they would not have exhibited to a middle class English sociologist. The success of his opening gambit, that he was in Britain to learn something of the problems of factory life that would be useful when introducing mechanisation into Pakistan, itself could form an interesting anthropological study. The trade union officials with whom he came into contact went out of their way to pass him on to their colleagues; at no time in the course of his investigations did he find himself short of persons to interview.

It is explained later how he classified the material that he obtained in this way, but for the moment it is enough to say that these three statements each represent a meaning that was again and again conveyed by the voluntary remarks of the factory workers. The words used would, of course, vary from occasion to occasion, but each of these statements is typical of the family it represents. Hence it is to be expected that, if these statements were read by the employees of a factory similar to any of those in which the free interviews had been conducted, they would be meaningful to the readers. Some might naturally disagree with one or more of them; the fact that a statement is intelligible does not mean that one agrees with it. In fact, these three statements were printed (together with 31 others) on a standard questionnaire, and those interviewed were invited to respond to each statement in any one of five ways:

SA = strongly agree

A = agree or tend to agree

U = uncertain or cannot understand

D = disagree or tend to disagree

SD = strongly disagree.

No respondent could possibly be aware of how any other completed the instrument, since all were met in conditions of confidence and noncollusiveness. We proceed to analyse the responses secured from one particular factory, identified here as M.

4. Some Responses of Factory M

In M there were about 2,000 persons altogether employed; in the sample of 85 interviewed, 42 were ordinary shop floor workers, 16 were supervisors, either foremen or charge hands, 27 were shop stewards or other elected representatives. Each of these 85 men gave responses to the 34 statements, thus supplying 2,890 pieces of information. For the present we consider only the 255 responses to the three statements set out above.

We note firstly that, since the study was of communications, the 42 shop floor workers and the 27 shop stewards were asked to give their own responses to the statements, while the 16 supervisors were asked to give not their own responses, *but those of the shop floor workers as the supervisors thought those responses to be.* The supervisors were thus returning not their own opinions, but their perceptions of the opinions of the workmen of whom they were in charge. If communications were perfect, it would be expected that, allowing for the fact that there are bound to be differences between individuals within any class (for example, that the 42 workmen would not all give the same responses as each other), there would be no significant differences between the average views of workmen and of shop stewards, nor between these and the perceptions that the supervisors had of the views of those who worked under them.

We note secondly that all the three statements have the same direction; agreement with any of them as they stand suggests a point of view that is "morally right", or that would at least attract social approval. The first remark, for example, suggests that, if the men keep their bargain, the management are decent enough to respect their integrity; the second implies that it is an offence against society to try to get something for nothing, or that no gentleman tries to take from the common fund more than he puts into it; the third suggests that there is a recognition of the responsibility that all members of the group carry for completing the task. To disagree with any of the statements implies either that the foremen are slavedrivers, that slacking can be indulged in without harmful effect or that there is no common purpose shared by men and management.

The simplest test of whether or not the three classes of employee give similar responses to the three statements, themselves comprising an expression of the degree of integration of the working team, is to be found by examining Table I, setting out these responses.

Number and Class of Respondents	Class of Response				
	SA	A	U	D	SD
16 F	10	11	6	15	6
42 W	16	42	14	35	19
27 S	7	36	10	22	6
85 All	33	89	30	72	31

Table I, showing the distribution, by five levels of agreement, of the responses of 16 supervisors, 42 workmen and 27 shop stewards to three statements about factory team work.

The distribution of opinion recorded in Table I shows no significant difference whatever between the three classes of employee. The balance of agreement and disagreement at both levels, is the same among shop stewards as among workmen, and is perceived by the supervisors to be the same among them as is expressed by the men themselves.* Whatever may be this

*For 8 degrees of freedom the value of x^2 for the hypothesis that the three rows of figures of Table I are drawn from the same population is 9·35. There is a 40% chance of finding a value of x^2 at least as large as this by random chance.

balance of opinion between agreement and disagreement it is to all intent and purpose the same among the men and their shop stewards, and is accurately perceived by their foremen. No communication problem is thus suggested, at least between classes; there are, of course, considerable disagreements between individuals within classes.

It is interesting to examine the balance of opinion itself. Although there are 122 responses expressing agreement and only 103 expressing disagreement, the difference of 19 is not significant. In other words the total view of these three statements—or of the factory condition that these statements suggest—is of neutrality. There is no decisive feeling that the factory is a place to bring out high principles, on the one hand, nor is there a cynical acceptance of low standards, on the other. Studies in other factories show that the average attitudes of the men can be significantly different, both much higher and much lower; Factory M is, among all those examined, a good average, at least in these views of the employees upon the quality of its teamwork.

5. Some Different Responses at Factory M

But consider now the responses of the men and of their shop stewards, and the perceptions held by the supervisors of the views of the men, not of something as general as the team spirit in the factory, but of so specific a matter as work study. If work study means anything, it means the possibility of change, the likelihood that different things will be done or that the same things will be done differently. Typical remarks passed about work study during the free interviews include the following:

"In this firm the men get as much out of work study as do the management."

"Work study makes plenty of jobs and a full order book."

"Getting work study into the factory creates more trouble for the men than it is worth."

We note that the third of these statements has a direction

different from the other two, in that agreement with it suggests disapproval or hostility. Hence, in any attempt to use the responses of the three classes of employee as an indication of their outlook towards work study, it is necessary to count agreements with the third statement among disagreements with the other two and vice versa. When this is done we obtain Table II.

Number and Class of Respondents	Class of Response				
	SA	A	U	D	SD
16 F	10	26	6	3	3
42 W	9	51	29	22	15
27 S	5	16	11	23	26
85 All	24	93	46	48	44

Table II, showing, by five levels of agreement, the distribution of the responses of 16 supervisors, 42 workmen and 27 shop stewards, towards three statements about work study.

The distribution of the 255 responses among the entries of Table II differs significantly from that of Table I. The supervisors, for example, record 36 favourable perceptions of the men's views against 6 unfavourable, a ratio of 6 to 1 for work study. The men themselves are certainly favourable, but in the proportion of 60 to 37 only; the shop stewards are opposed in the ratio of 7 to 3 against. The distributions of opinion differ so markedly between the three classes of employee that it is quite out of the question to suggest that, basically, there is the same unanimity as is expressed in Table I about the team spirit as a whole, but that the scores actually recorded in Table II are the chance fluctuations that one must come to expect when trying to measure so variable a quality as human opinion.* We must

*For 8 degrees of freedom the value x^2 for the hypothesis that the three rows of figures of Table II are drawn from the same population is 46·5. The probability of a value as large as this being found by random chance is entirely negligible ($x^2 = 26 \cdot 12$ for p = 0·1%).

therefore accept the view that the differences expressed by the three classes of men are caused, or that they can be traced to assignable reasons. However concordant may be the views of the three classes of men in such general matters as the quality of the esprit-de-corps within the factory, there are real and sharp divergences of view upon the acceptability of such positive action as the introduction of work study. Such attempts to measure the managerial climate reveal that, intermingled with a balanced and concordant view of the general relations between men and management, there can exist the greatest disparities of outlook upon such fundamental matters as the ethical value of industrial change. It is these contradictions and complexities that impoverish our understanding of factory behaviour; a general indication of goodwill, or at least of lack of hostility, may be no indication whatever that, on specific matters, there is any common view, whether favourable or not. For the manager the problem is not so much that the men are, in the proportion of about 3 to 2 against, unsympathetic towards work study; his difficulty is introduced by the false perception of his supervisors, who see the men as overwhelmingly favourable, and in the exaggerated hostility of the shop stewards, who bring to their negotiations a set of attitudes more negative than those of the men they purport to represent.

6. The Wider Measurement of Attitudes

Since there appears to be no difficulty in securing responses of the kind here illustrated, it may well be possible to adapt such statements to cataloguing the attitudes of representative samples of employees; the battery that has been assembled during the present research can be completed within a quarter of an hour, even although several man-years of work have gone into compiling it in the first instance. In the course of this research many thousands of remarks have been passed about work study in its infinite variety of aspects. But it has been possible to classify most of these under a comparatively few specific headings, each of which can be represented by a statement such as one of the two sets of three whose responses are analysed in Tables I and II. Such headings, to be regarded as satisfactory, need to satisfy several conditions; it is, for example, a waste of time to invite the opinions of workpeople upon questions of general agreement, such as the opinion, volunteered over and over again, that piece rate schemes threaten the maintenance of high quality. The most satisfactory headings are those that discriminate strongly between one factory and another, or, within the same factory, between one group and another. The feature of any instrument of investigation that measures its relevance to the task in hand is the extent to which it discriminates between one investigated situation and another. It is the valuable property of litmus to turn either red or blue that makes it valuable as an indicator for acids and alkalis; it would be useless if it gave the same response to both. Likewise with the research statement; the responses to it must depend critically upon the atmosphere within the factory.

Secondly, the number of statements in the battery must not be so great that men lose interest in responding to them. Nor, indeed, must the research worker assemble more data than he can reasonably handle. In the present research 34 statements were eventually chosen as representative of those aspects of the factory climate in which we had become interested; it was possible, or appeared subjectively possible, to classify the bulk of the many thousands of remarks, prejudices, anecdotes, myths, rumours and opinions under 34 headings. Each of these were then represented by one statement, and six examples of the 34 statements have already been given.

Thirdly, it is desirable, to simplify yet further the task of making meaningful this mass of data—for in one use alone of these methods described lower down 9,078 responses were collected—to be able to break the 34 remarks down into a small number of wider classes. In the present research, concerned mainly with attitudes to work study, three such wider classes were built into the structure of the survey instruments: attitudes to work study as such; attitudes to management; attitudes to the existing working conditions that the new methods would be expected to change. These three sub-classes are, of course, not imported into the thousands of original opinions, nor into the 34 headings under which they were classified. It might be less inaccurate to say that it is possible to classify the 34 statements (and so the masses of opinions they represent) in such a way that those most loaded with views about management fall into one sub-class, those most loaded with views about work study into a second; and those most loaded with views about the status quo into a third. But none of these sub-classes are pure, nor can they be. Management must inevitably be perceived in its attitudes towards work study; the status quo, too, must be seen in such a piece of research in relation to the work study that is being engineered to threaten it. However this may be, the 34 remarks were, for some purposes, treated as three sub-classes; in sub-class A, there were 8 statements about management; in sub-class B, 14 statements about work study; in sub-class C, 12 statements about conditions already existing in the factory. A list of the 34 separate subjects is given in the Appendix; six of the 34 statements are, of course, already disclosed in Paras. 4 and 5 above.

Fourthly, and most important of all, the use of the battery must produce results that have undeniable statistical significance. Their use must produce more than a mass of responses to statements that are syntactically unobjectionable; they must pretend to more than mere face-validity. The battery chosen must produce responses from a sample of men so that—

(a) whatever the response of any particular individual to any particular statement, there must be revealed a consistency about his total responses that is different from that of others responding under the same conditions; and

(b) whatever the response of any particular individual to any particular statement, all the individuals within the set responding tend to give a similar response to the same statement, suggesting a consistency of opinion upon that statement throughout the whole set, a consistency differ-

ent from that of the total responses to some other
statement.

The battery must, in the jargon of statistics, reveal significantly greater variations between men, on the one hand, and between statements, on the other, than the random or residual
variations introduced by particular men when confronted with
particular statements. If the variations between men and statements are no greater than these adventitious variations the
battery is worthless. We proceed at once to examine this point.

7. The Use of Quantitative Methods

We may assume that the response of each man to any particular
statement implies a relation to his total factory experience. This
relation may be regarded, to a first approximation, as a point
upon a line of finite length. One end of the line represents un-
qualified hostility, at which point the man will no longer be able
to endure what the factory has to offer and will try to get away
under any conditions. The other end of the line represents
unreserved satisfaction, at which point it would be virtually
impossible to persuade the man to spend his life occupied elsewhere. Factories with high labour turnover would tend to find
their men's opinions towards the first end of the line; and vice
versa. The model is, of course, intended to help the analysis
of the present data; it does not pretend to represent the complexities of the real situation.

But it would be fair to suggest that the man who responded to
the 34 statement battery with 34 strongly expressed anti-social
views would be at a point on this scale a long way from the man
whose 34 opinions were all strongly oriented to co-operation and
friendliness. In fact no man of the several hundred who completed the battery showed views anything like so consistently
one way or the other. But to make progress we may suggest that
each of the 34 statements is either positive or negative; positive
statements are such that agreement with them implies satisfaction or fairness; negative statements are such that to agree with

them one sees either an unsatisfactory state of affairs around one or that one is charged with selfish or anti-social views. We may return to the two statements—

"So long as you get your fair day's work done, the foreman does not bother you."

"Getting work study into the factory creates more trouble for the men than it is worth."

and observe that agreement with the first suggests satisfaction with the management's interpretation of the wages bargain, whereas disagreement implies that, on this matter at least, the management is not fair. Suppose then that the responses are translated into numbers; we award +2 for strong agreement, +1 for agreement or a tendency to it, o for uncertainty, −1 for disagreement or a tendency to it, −2 for strong disagreement. But agreement with the second suggests a concealed dissatisfaction—and it may not be deeply concealed. In the same way, therefore, we might award −2 for strong agreement with the second statement, −1 for agreement or a tendency to it, o for uncertainty, +1 for disagreement or a tendency to it, and +2 for strong disagreement.

We may then analyse the 2,890 responses of the 85 employees of Factory M according to these numerically allocated scores. The results are given in Table III.

Number and class of Respondents	+2	+1	o	−1	−2
16 F	138	235	45	93	33
42 W	171	518	220	314	205
27 S	64	336	86	293	139
85 All	373	1,089	351	700	377

Table III, showing by numerical scores, the responses of 85 employees of Factory M to a battery of 34 statements.

From Table III it may be shown that the grand total for all 2,890 responses is $+381$, giving an average positive mark for each man-response of $0 \cdot 1318$; on this scale subjective agreement to any positive statement is awarded unity. This average is significantly greater than zero, showing that the overall score, for Factory M, suggests an esprit-de-corps slightly more positive than neutrality. For the 42 workmen taken alone the corresponding mean is $+0 \cdot 0952$; this may be compared to $-0 \cdot 0982$ in a second factory and $+0 \cdot 4241$ in a third. These differences are highly significant. We also observe that Table III resembles Table II more than it does Table I, namely, that, overall, supervisors' perceptions of what the men think and feel are grossly optimistic and the views expressed by the shop stewards significantly less favourable than those by the men themselves.

8. The Pervasiveness of Attitudes and Personalities of Individuals

Having now suggested how the responses of the individual to the statement can be measured, we may now test whether—

(a) particular individuals, however varied the statements they are scoring, tend always to display their own individuality; and

(b) each particular statement tends to display its own level of acceptability, positive or negative, pervading the group of individuals who score it, however much these individuals may differ from each other.

Since we know that for this purpose the foremen, the workmen and the shop stewards may give significantly different responses, we must test the two propositions above three times. The results are that, within each of these three classes, the men display marked individual responses, and that each of the three classes of men, taken together, shows significant differences between its 34 particular statements. The evidence is given in Table IV, analysing the variance of the three families of scores into that between individuals, that between statements and the residual variance to be accounted for by the vast number of accidental and non-assignable sources. No man is ever, nor can be, wholly consistent in expressing two successive opinions, let alone 34; no single statement can ever command a unanimous response from all to whom it is put, particularly a statement that is bound to touch upon the relations between the respondents. But the questions are whether the degrees of consistency in the responses outweigh these random variations, and whether the ratio is so great as to reveal beyond doubt that such consistencies exist.

Source of Variation	Sum of Squares	Degrees of Freedom	Estimate of Variance	F
Between supervisors ..	107	15	7·13	6·27
Between statements ..	114	33	3·45	3·03
Residual ..	563	495	1·14	—
Between workmen ..	365	41	8·90	7·24
Between statements ..	289	33	8·76	7·12
Residual ..	1,669	1,353	1·23	—
Between shop stewards	236	26	9·08	7·76
Between statements ..	191	33	5·78	4·94
Residual ..	1,002	858	1·17	—

Table IV, showing for three classes of employee in Factory M, the analysis of variance of responses to 34 statements. In all six cases, the value of F is greater than would have occurred by chance once in ten thousand times.

We see from Table IV that the three estimates of the residual variances are of the same order; the causes of scatter around the individual consistencies of men and topics are much the same for foremen, workmen and shop stewards. But in all cases the variance ratios set out in the table are significantly greater than could have possibly occurred by chance. In other words the differences between the individual men within each group are real, and do not depend upon these chance variations; so also are the group responses to the single statements significantly different among themselves.

We can go further than this. The variance among the supervisors, $7 \cdot 13$, does not differ from that among the workmen, $8 \cdot 90$, nor from that among the shop stewards, $9 \cdot 08$. In other words, whatever are the causes at work among a group of shop stewards to give them each their individual slant upon any factory topic that comes before them, these causes produce a variety of slants to no significant extent different from the variety of slants among the workmen or among the supervisors. This is merely to prove the obvious, perhaps, although it may not be so regarded: the *scatter* of personality is just the same among each random sample of men, even although the average measure of one sample may differ from the average of another.*

But we are not solely concerned with the individualities of the employees, nor even within the scatter within groups of them. Our interest is in their opinions towards factory topics. To what extent do the shop stewards or the supervisors exhibit the same patterns of response as do the workmen for whom they claim to speak or whom they pretend to control? It has already been shown that on some topics the views expressed by the three parties are consonant while on others they diverge significantly. Table IV shows that, in the supervisor group the variance between topics is $3 \cdot 45$; in the workmen group it is $8 \cdot 76$. In other words the supervisors tend to see much less variety between the workmen's responses to the statements than do the workmen themselves. The difference is highly significant, showing what might be expected, namely, that the supervisors tend to overlay the sharp differences seen by the men themselves with their common view as supervisors. They tend to report (even although each supervisor in so reporting expresses his individual slant) a generalised view of what they feel the men believe, a view that takes the contrasts off the men's true opinions of this, that and

*A class of seven year old children will be taller, on average, than a class of six year olds. But the scatters within each class will not be significantly different.

the other. They see their men through spectacles with lenses of frosted glass.

Likewise there is a difference between the variances among the statements made by shop stewards, on the one hand, and among the statements made by the workmen, on the other. But the two variances are not significantly different, although the direction (8·76 among the workmen's responses to the 34 statements against 5·78 among those of the shop stewards) suggests that there is also a tendency for the shop stewards to see each topic in the same way, and not as sharply contrasted, one topic against another, as do the men. This again, is a conclusion to be expected. But the fact that it appears, like that of the foremen's stronger loss of definition, should increase our confidence in the methods by which it has been reached.

9. The Differences between Factories

Whatever may be the powers of statistical discrimination revealed by surveys of this type, their value must in the end by judged by the ability of management to use them for improving the

Factory	No. of Respondents	Mean Score for 34 items	Mean Item Score A	B	C
N	31	14·419	0·432	0·038	0·894
K	27	11·593	0·477	0·196	0·392
G	39	9·615	0·237	0·269	0·340
L	40	4·850	0·012	−0·023	0·235
M	42	3·238	−0·006	0·056	0·210
H	26	1·154	0·039	0·027	0·045
J	62	−3·339	−0·141	−0·248	0·108

Table V, showing various numerical scores suggesting responses of 267 shop floor workers in seven factories towards statements about factory life.

conditions within their own enterprises. But before this can be done, the individual factory must display what, in terms of this survey, are its weak points. Hence it is in the use of these methods to compare one factory with another that their practical value, if any, may reside. We give an example of such application forthwith.

At seven factories a random sample of men, the smallest of 26, the largest of 62, were invited to complete the battery. The results are shown in Table V. This gives, factory by factory, the number of men completing the survey, their average scores for all 34 statements taken together, and their average scores per item in the three sub-classes (A, management; B, work study; C, existing conditions).

The distribution of the scores of the individual men, 31 in N, and 62 in J, on the 12 statements about existing conditions is shown in Fig. I; we note that the average difference is about

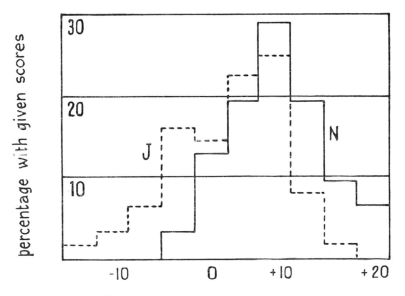

FIG. I, showing distribution of attitudes towards working conditions in two different factories, J and N.

three quarters of a grade. We must first ask whether the differences between the factories suggested by these scores are significant, that is, whether there is a tendency for some factories to score more than others that could not, given the known differences between the 267 individuals whose responses have been collected, have occurred by chance. If it did not so occur, it must have been caused and the causes should be assignable. The question may be answered by analysing the variance of the 267 scores, between the seven factories and within them. The results are given in Table VI.

Source of Variation	Sum of Squares	Degrees of Freedom	Estimate of Variance	F
Between factories ..	9,573	6	1,595	6·54
Within factories ..	63,376	260	243·8	

Table VI, showing the analysis of variance of responses of 267 men to 34 statements, the men being drawn in random samples from seven factories.

For 6 and 260 degrees of freedom, the 1 % and 0·1 % values of F are 2·92 and 4·00 respectively. It is thus impossible to overlook the great differences between the scores of the men in the seven factories; in some the overall average scores are very significantly greater than are those in others.

Nor is this all. Factories N, K and G appear to return scores significantly higher than those from the other factories, with the exception of the score suggesting attitudes to work study (B) at factory N. It might well be asked whether, with so outstandingly favourable an expression of attitudes towards existing conditions (C), it would be expected that the men would want to support work study. However this may be, we may test the differences between the 97 men as a whole at factories N, K and G, on the one hand, and the 170 as a whole at the four others. The mean of the 97 men is 11·701 for all 34 items; of the 170 others it is 0·900. The standard deviation of the individual scores is 16·53. The difference between the two means is 10·801, and their standard deviation 2·10. Since the difference is over 5 times the standard deviation it is highly significant; we conclude that the scores of the 97 men at N, K and G are drawn from a population different from the 170 others. Since N, K and G belong to the same firm, but are widely scattered territorially we reach the interesting result that the scores at N, K or G are in some way a reflection of a set of attitudes that manage to pervade the whole firm, even though its factories are scattered through different counties.

10. The Homogeneity of the Group

We may at once test to what extent there is any difference in the averages of the three sets of scores of the men in the three factories, N, G and K. The variance analysis is given in Table VII.

Source of Variation	Sum of Squares	Degrees of Freedom	Estimate of Variance	F
Between factories ..	399	2	199·5	1·14
Within factories ..	21,453	94	228·2	

Table VII, showing the analysis of variance of the responses of 97 men to 34 statements, the men being drawn in random samples from three associated factories.

For three factories and 97 men the variance ratio should be at least 1·64 for even a 20 % likelihood that there are differences between the factories. There is thus no evidence whatever to suggest that the average responses differ between the three factories. Judged by their responses to these statements the total scores of the men towards the subjects touched upon are the same, on average, in all the factories of the group; the differences observed, such as they are, can readily be explained by the natural differences between individual men and there are no detectable factory influences affecting all the men in any one of the factory group differently from those in any other. Since none of the 97 men who scored the 34 item survey in any of the three factories had ever worked in any other factory of the group, this result is an impressive verification of the theory that influences can be transmitted between factories through their mere membership of the same organisation; the transmission mechanism must be some quality of central management readily sensed by those locally in charge of the operating units.

We may follow this suggestion up by examining the differences between the other four factories. Since these belong to four different firms and thus are not subjected to any overall unifying influences we should expect significant differences between them. This turns out to be so, although admittedly not by any emphatic margin. The analysis of variance is given in Table VIII.

Source of Variation	Sum of Squares	Degrees of Freedom	Estimate of Variance	F
Between factories ..	1,969	3	656·3	2·60
Within factories ..	41,918	166	252·1	

Table VIII, showing the analysis of variance of the responses of 170 men to 34 statements, the men being drawn in random samples from four unassociated factories.

For four factories and 170 men the variance ratio of 2·60 is significant at 5 %. It is thus likely that the four factories differ among themselves in the sense that their employees do not have, on average, the same views upon the subjects touched upon in the survey. For all that, the differences between the total responses at the four factories are not so different as to prevent us from considering them as a control against which to examine the undoubtedly superior responses of the 97 men in the three associated factories, N, K and G. Is it possible to draw any general conclusions about the 267 men as a whole? Is it possible, by contrasting the 97 in the three associated factories with the

170 in the four, item by item over the whole 34, to suggest in what the strength of the group of three consists, and where, if at all, it compares unfavourably?

11. Group of Three and Non-Group of Four

We may, for each of 34 items, write down the total score of the 97 men in the group of three factories, and the total score of 170 in the non-group of four. These are shown on Fig. II. The correlation coefficient is $+0 \cdot 747$ and is so significant that it could

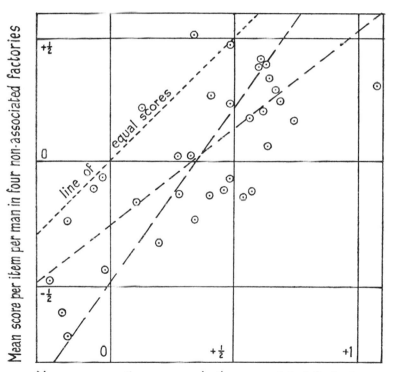

Mean score per item per man in three associated factories

FIG. II, showing systematic score difference between factories.

not possibly have occurred by chance. Thus, although the average performance of the four is so much more negative than that of the three, the relative scores of the individual items are correlated; items relatively favourably regarded in the three are, on the whole, relatively favourably regarded in the four, although with a significantly lesser degree of favour. This is perhaps not surprising; the relative choices of a sample of a hundred men on matters fundamental to those men would not change out of all recognition with their environment. Even in a very good group men still respect their union; even when men earn high wages they still feel it unfair that old men should have to accept the same piece rates as their sons. It is merely that the general level of intensity of all their feelings moves up or moves down. Sweetness, when it pervades one point of view, seems to a significant extent, to pervade all, but the all-pervading sweetness of one factory may be easier to detect than that of another.

The correlation is naturally not perfect. On some items the difference between the factories does not follow the general rule. Some points on the scatter diagram of Fig. II are further from the trends than others. It is fairly easy to show, since each point contrasts the views of 97 men in the three associated factories with those of 170 in another four in no way related, that the views of the 97 are in some cases significantly *less* favourable than those of the 170, even although, taking all 34 views together, they are on average much more so. It comes out clearly that the men in the group of three factories feel strongly that work study may deprive their tasks of interest, that the changes of method it may bring are bound to increase the effort needed to earn bonus and that there is a danger of the production processes being held up by shortages should new methods be introduced. On all other matters their views are more favourable than those of the men in the other four factories; it should thus be of interest to their group management to reflect upon the possible causes of this significant difference. It may, of course, reflect some unfortunate work study policy of the past when too-hasty an attempt to change traditional practice was made. It is of no less interest to examine in what respect the scores of the men in the group of three factories, although on average better, are best of all. It is on the item "If the boss wants anything done here, he expects us to put up ideas." The score of the 97 workmen in the three factories averages $1 \cdot 103$ per man; for the 170 in the four it is $0 \cdot 353$. In the three factories the averages are $0 \cdot 923$, $1 \cdot 111$ and $1 \cdot 323$ respectively; in the four they are $-0 \cdot 154$, $0 \cdot 629$, $0 \cdot 275$ and $0 \cdot 286$ respectively. Remembering the large numbers of men for whom these averages are drawn, it is clear that in the three factories the men feel that they are genuinely expected to contribute when they can; in the four they are unable to feel so. Other researches suggest a simple explanation: if the managers of the three are each encouraged to put up suggestions to their central office, they will in turn encourage their own subordinates to supply them with ideas to pass on. It has been shown, for example, that nurses who are encouraged by their doctors to make suggestions about patient care tend to be more communicative with the patients themselves.

It may also be helpful to the central management of the three factories to know in which aspect of factory life the men display the greatest differences of outlook. The factory averages that differed most turned out to be the men's responses to the statement about physical surroundings; "The last thing thought about here is the comfort of those who do the work". Where one higher management controls the working conditions of three factories it may be of interest for them to know of any differences of view between the men in them, especially if these differences are not (as they often are not) visible in the form of canteen, lighting or other common amenities. It is, or should by now be, well known that complaints about the environment are frequently the expression of hostility to something deeper. The second subject of greatest inter-factory variation was the benefits derived from work study; in one factory there was a strong opinion that these went to the management rather than to the men. But we repeat the general conclusion: the average scores of all three factories were similar and they were much higher than those of the other four. It is only to press the data as far as possible to search for the relative imperfections among what is undoubtedly a satisfactory group taken all in all.

12. Conclusion

We have developed an instrument for assessing the outlooks of those on the factory floor upon a range of topics that appear to them to be important. This survey instrument produces results that can be shown, by the methods of statistics, to have significant implications; to discriminate between one workman's outlook and that of another; to show that men feel more sympathetic or more hostile about some topics than about others; that the overall outlooks of some factories may be substantially better or worse than the overall outlooks of others. It shows that common view points may pervade a group of factories run by one central management, but situated at great distances from each other, suggesting that communications are effective in moulding attitudes without those persons who share the attitudes needing to meet face to face. Such an instrument can be applied to a sample of men in a factory in half an hour; it could be scored, analysed and, at least in terms of its immediate contents, interpreted within 24 hours, if there were a desire to do so. While it is not suggested that, independently of all other information about the behaviour of the workmen, the results of the instrument must necessarily give the management new insight into some of their shop floor relationships, they might raise questions of interest that had not been raised before.

It is often said that a deeper understanding of industrial morale is of no consequence unless it can be so used as to raise productivity or to lower costs or to produce some other measurable economic gain. It is, indeed, symptomatic of our present machine-and-money culture to expect that any improvement in industrial relations ought to lead to an improvement in efficiency. There is, of course, no reason why a more friendly acceptance of management's proposals should not inspire extra effort, but, on the other hand, a more relaxed atmosphere in the workshop may be a worthwhile end in itself, without necessarily having to identify it in terms of productivity. Society is a better place if a miner produces ten tons of coal in a shift without anxiety, without aggression towards his supervisors, without the constant wish that he were elsewhere, than if, during the same task, he is worried about his working conditions, is in perpetual conflict with his management, and is looking eagerly forward to his escape from the pit. In our constant preoccupation with what is called our standard of living we are apt to forget that the work by which we earn that living is part of it; any improvement in the state of mind in which we do that work is, irrespective of additional economic gain, an increment in our living standards. Perhaps the investigation of how we actually feel at work, as distinct from how our betters think we feel, or how we ought to feel, opens up prospects of understanding that could also rate high in pecuniary terms. What is it worth, to management and to men alike, that a less inexact view of our feelings is made possible?

Appendix

List of 34 "factory-topics" raised by Lancashire workmen in volunteering views about work study. These are not in order of importance nor of the frequency with which they were volunteered.

A. Mainly about management

Management's tendency to take decisions before listening to workmen.

Management's willingness to clear up difficulties felt by workmen.

Supervisor's consideration of possible future problems.

Supervisor's non-interference with capable workmen.

Management's willingness to introduce improvements without union pressure to do so.

Management's ability to listen to suggestions from subordinates.

Supervisor's reluctance to change workmen's task without notice or discussion.

Supervisor's expectation that workmen will make suggestions about methods to be used on new jobs.

B.   Mainly about work study

Workers' share of benefits compared with those of management.

Magnitude of teething troubles on introducing change.

Fairness in allocation of good and bad jobs.

Extent to which bonus keeps pace with output.

Flexibility of scheme in allowing workmen to make good week's earnings if so disposed.

Experience in job itself of work study engineer who introduces it.

Extent to which new method deprives job of interest.

Extent to which bonus scheme rewards good worker relative to the poor.

Fairness or otherwise of scheme in not penalising the older worker.

Confidence that good performance will not lead to cuts in the rate.

Belief that effective work study leads to fuller order book.

Extent to which earnings may temporarily suffer when new methods are introduced.

Confidence that any new bonus scheme contains adequate safeguards against loss through waiting time and other operational shortcomings.

Confidence that times can be fairly measured and need not be guessed.

C.   Mainly about existing work conditions

Effect of one slacker on success of group.

Satisfaction with existing rates of earnings.

Confidence that all employees are treated alike.

Security in employment as affected by productivity of firm.

Manifestation of team spirit at place of work.

Confidence in Works Council as an instrument for resolving problems.

Extent to which shop floor puts forward new ideas that are considered.

Confidence that workmen will not be arbitrarily shifted from one job to another.

Attractiveness of physical surroundings.

Adequacy of tools and so forth at start of any new job.

Adequacy of supply and maintenance services.

Satisfaction that workmen's abilities are recognised and fully used.

It is clear that each one of these subjects is of considerable complexity and strongly loaded with elements of others. This comes out in the correlation between the scores of men when these are given numerical values. Such correlation does not, of course, affect the conclusion that there are highly significant differences between the average outlooks of men in different factories.

DECISIONS, COMMUNICATIONS AND MORALE

Decisions as the central activity of managers

Managers spend much of their time preparing for, taking or putting into effect decisions. It is, of course, true that all intelligent behaviour, whether of persons who call themselves managers or not, demands the taking of decisions, and even that quite complicated decisions may be taken by animals, as one may observe in a cat preparing to take evasive action on seeing a dog. But there is (or should be) a deliberateness, or even a detachment, about the decisions of a professional manager that gives them a character and an interest of their own. Managers, whose principal task is to make up their minds, will often (unlike the cat) deliberately decide long in advance upon the future sequence of decisions in which they will be engaged; they do not always wait until the emergency suddenly forces itself upon their attention. They can, moreover, communicate to other managers the need for decisions to be taken, often in accordance with quite elaborate rules.

There are three broad types of decisions. The first have a fixed and identifiable criterion of choice, and may, at first sight, seem to demand little intelligence. Should, for example, such-and-such a person be admitted to a football game as a spectator?

If he holds a ticket for a reserved seat or has the money to buy one the answer is, presumably, Yes. If he has no ticket or no money (and no influence) the answer is, presumably, No. But a decision as to whether or not such-and-such a person should be admitted to a hospital may be more complicated, although logically still a Yes or No choice. The second class of decisions demand a discrimination between several alternatives, each of which is determined in advance. The football spectator may, for example, need to be admitted not merely to the ground as a whole but to a particular stand or part of the ground; the choice for the patient may not be a simple Yes or No about admission to hospital, but a choice between many different wards in accordance with his particular diagnostic group. The question is not simply whether some specified criterion is met or not, but which particular criterion of several that might be expected. The third class of decisions are not (either wholly or partly) determined by previously known or specifiable criteria, and require, in making them, that their criteria shall be, to some extent, selected with the decisions themselves. The managers, (or gatekeepers) at the football ground may, for example, be faced firstly with the "admit or exclude" decision; secondly, after admission to the ground, with the multiple choice of which particular section of the ground; and thirdly, with a choice not in any way officially laid down in advance, such as whether, for a small bribe or other consideration, to give the spectator a seat within range of the television cameras, or that brings him close to distinguished visitors, or even enables him to stage an outburst on behalf of a political cause at some crucial point of the game. In this third choice the decision would explicitly recognise the acceptance of an unofficial payment as a criterion to be observed or not, even although the subsequent behaviour of the spectator could not, it is supposed, be known fully in advance; as in all decisions of the third class the man who introduces unprogrammed criteria must reckon with unexpected outcomes. It is normally the aim of managers to keep these to a minimum although at times trial decisions are taken by managers who know perfectly well that they are acting in the dark and must be prepared for almost anything. Such will be the surgeon who decides to open a patient up in the hope that he will thereby discover more about his condition and perhaps even be able to treat him inside the second class of decision, namely, by carrying out some standard operation to be selected in the light of further knowledge; the surgeon may, of course, find that the patient's precise condition is still obscure or cannot be treated by any straightforward procedure already known to his team. In practice, it is decisions of the third type, in which the goals themselves have to be sought (as well as the means of reaching them) that are of greatest interest both to managers and to students of management.

The structure of decisions

Insofar as decisions are deliberative (that is, not the mere outcome of pure chance, as in copying the spin of a roulette wheel or the flight of pigeons) they exhibit a common structure. All intelligent behaviour presupposes a goal, objective, aim, profit, pay off or utility, since the decision taker has a reason for his behaviour and expects some gain from it; secondly, he must overcome some obstruction, difficulty, problem, obstacle or disadvantage in order to achieve that gain, for if nothing stood between him and his goals he would have no need to take decisions; thirdly, the decision taker must have certain resources at his disposal in order to overcome his problem and reach his goal. These three elements—utility, problem and resource—are common to all decisions. The manager cannot, of course, work with these three elements directly; he may not even see his physical resources. He works in information about the three elements and insofar as his information is correct his decisions (if intelligently taken) will be satisfactory. If his information is inaccurate (however intelligently it is used) his decisions will be poor; it is impossible, except occasionally and then by pure chance, for decisions to be better than the information available to the manager who uses it.

It is the role of operational research to suggest to managers in situations of complexity what information they need to specify their goals, problems and resources, once the management have suggested in what direction they would like their goals to be found. The final choice of goal depends upon final values, and this is an absolute choice on which the advice of an operational research worker, however competent, is of no more value than the advice of any other person. But once management has selected its goals (perhaps after a brief study of its present situation, to review or evaluate what goals might be attainable) the processes of decision taking become the assembly and treatment of information about these goals, about the problems that stand in the way of their achievement, and about the resources needed to solve these problems. If this information can be expressed in clear terms it may well be that an exact decision can be taken, and that, for the goals selected by the management, this decision may be the best possible. A typical goal might be the minimisation of some set of distribution costs; the management would need to define what is meant by the concept of a minimum, but, given this, and such information as the addresses of the warehouses and customers, the length and condition of the roads between them and the nature and volume of the goods to be sent, on the one hand, and, on the other, the costs, both capital and operational, of the transport fleet, the management could reach a definite decision. Its accuracy would naturally depend upon the accuracy of the information available and upon the computational facilities that the management could command. But there would be no need to invoke guesswork nor intuition; the decision could be taken from logical first principles once the primary goals had been declared, the task specified and the resources catalogued. In theory, the information necessary for these three steps should be both accessible and clear.

Subjective decisions

In practice the task of the decision taker may be more difficult,

4

not only in degree, but in dimension. To begin with, the manager is a human being, and the goals, problems and resources that he perceives in taking his decisions are influenced, perhaps strongly, by his personality, his past experience, his personal expectations of reward and the customs and practices prevailing around him. Moreover, the information originally available to him may depend upon his personal relations with colleagues and subordinates; some of these may have their reasons either for telling him what they think he wants to know, whatever the truth; others may tell him only what they want him to know; others may tell him next to nothing; others, while not consciously misleading him, may make his task more difficult than it need be by some lack of frankness in saying what they have to say; others may consciously mislead him. It may well be that all or most of these infelicities of communication derive in part from a coldness in the manager himself; they may surround his office. But taken together they will obscure his goals, magnify his problems and cause him falsely to estimate his resources.

And even where there is no impediment of speech nor obliquity of vision, it may well be that decision taking, since it involves many persons, involves also just as many perceptions of goals, problems and resources. For example, in the commonest management structure, the manager works through his supervisors to direct and control the men who operate the productive machines and processes; the structure is three stage, but each stage may have its own ideas about goals, about problems and about available resources. A manager may not perceive that one of his most important goals is to heighten the self-respect of his subordinates (by adequate consultation before introducing change); or that one of his greatest problems is to know how the subordinates perceive their own problems; or that one of his richest potential resources are the unvoiced or neglected suggestions of his workmen. Social research discovers striking contradictions between the perceptions that the three levels have of these three elements of the total decision process; in many factories, too, there are significant differences between the views of the shop stewards, on the one hand, and of the men they represent, on the other.

Communication problems of large enterprises

The greater the distances between these three characteristic levels of the enterprise the greater may be the divergencies of view; to the policy maker the most pressing problem may be the difficulty of introducing a new product; to the manager in charge of the assembly line it may be the impossibility of balancing the line as it runs at present because of restrictive practices among the men; the principal complaint of these men may be that they are not permitted to agree among themselves how they might organise the existing flow more conveniently. As the levels recede from each other so does the difficulty of agreement about goals, problems or resources increase; the result is that management finds the workmen harder to control, the workmen find the management less easy to trust. The morale of the enterprise, defined as the willingness of all those employed in it, to agree upon and to help in achieving its collective aims, begins to suffer and may eventually so far decline that meaningful communication virtually ceases, and the authority of the management may collapse. This may be demonstrated by an analysis of the indicators of morale in enterprises of different sizes; disputes, absenteeism and accidents are relatively worse in the large concern, whether a factory, a coalmine or even a hospital. Averaged over an industry, the workmen in the large enterprise more readily mistrust the motives of their managements in appointing factory doctors than do the workmen in small; other things being equal, the resistance to change is greater in the large concern, and research shows that the resistance is not to change as such but to the management who are trying to introduce it. Research into attitudes and information flow suggests that, other things being equal, the large enterprise is faced with problems of learning and adjustment that do not arise in the small.

The growth of electronic computers has made possible new thinking about the nature of learning, loosely defined as any process of adjustment deriving wholly or mainly from within the learner. It is now demonstrable that learning is not the mere storage of new knowledge, but must include the re-arrangement of existing knowledge; it is also known that learning takes place only when the learner attempts, in some way, to use his newly arranged knowledge, and observes the success with which he does so. Learning, or the adjustment to new situations, therefore, demands that one shall know how one is getting on when one tries to apply what one is learning. This means that the learner shall have continuous knowledge of his own performance; one improves only by knowing one's successes and one's failures. The successful manager is thus aware of the effect he has on others while he tries to change the situation about him. The most important single quality of managers, which enables them continually to adjust to their surrounding world, is to know the impression that they make on their colleagues. The man who does not continually receive inputs about his own outputs, or who is not sensitive to the effect that he is having upon other persons, can never make a successful manager in situations of change. The more their world changes, demanding of managers new views of new goals, new solutions to new problems, and new uses for new resources, the greater is their need for unhindered communication with those who, in effecting or controlling change, are at work around them.

Rates of change

It is a commonplace that innovation is the most significant feature of modern life. It is not often appreciated *how* significant. Suppose that 20 years is the effective half life of the normal adult. In 1944 the maximum velocity of human travel was in the Mosquito aircraft, at 400 miles per hour. Today the space rocket is 50 times as fast. In 1923 the maximum velocity was nearly 200 miles per hour, or almost half the 1943 speed. The intensity of change, measured on this scale of simple dynamics, is thus 25 times greater in the second half of a present day manager's life than it was in the first. If the speed of development in data processing is assessed in the same way the development is even more impressive; the dynamics of the mind are coming to demand an athleticism no less intensive than that expected of the astronaut. The half life period is a useful estimate of the extent to which the present ideas of a normal man may be committed to the past; at the pace of present development some of the knowledge on which an engineering student is today examined for his degree will be obsolescent within ten years, and ludicrously out of date within twenty. But policy making managers tend to have graduated at least twenty years ago, and not infrequently they draw upon ideas now wholly with the dead and with the past. The ability to renounce one's intellectual inheritance is a precious accomplishment; misconceptions grow into personal beliefs and, like stained glass in an ancient cathedral, colour the sunlight of today with the unremembered intentions of yesterday. The teachings of Jesus Christ constantly refer to the need for simplicity of view, for the uncomplicated and for the uncommitted; "Blessed are the meek, for they shall inherit the earth"..... "Whosoever therefore shall humble himself as this little child, the same is greatest in the Kingdom of Heaven." All who have dealt with great men, such as Nobel prizewinners, must be impressed with their essential artlessness. Innovation is seen by them for what it is, and is not at once interpreted as something already familiar and thus already evaluated. This ability to free one's perception from irrelevant clutter may well be congenital, but it can be developed by the normal processes of learning. These depend upon one's capacity to sense the impression made on others by one's judgements and opinions, for it is these that reveal to others the shackles that are invisible to oneself. The sharpness of this impression depends largely upon one's capacity to listen, for it is by word of mouth that the majority of human beings exchange their impressions of each other. This capacity to listen can be developed by appropriate therapy; one form of this, vital to management education, is variously known as sensitivity training, group dynamics or N.T.L., attendance at a conference of the National Training Laboratory, an American teaching foundation. The significance of their work is the demonstration that, not only is discriminatory listening of cardinal importance to the manager, but that it can be taught to those who wish to learn. The manager who can listen, not only with courtesy, but also with patience to those who may seem to be attacking him, may learn something of great importance not only for himself but for his attackers. In any case, the success of any decision depends not only upon the "objective" information available to those called upon to make and implement it; the significance of this information to them in terms of goals, problems and resources is also important, and their perceptions of these may be strongly coloured by subjective but unsuspected elements. . . . . "For if thine eye be single thy whole body will be full of light. But if thine eye be evil, thy whole body will be full of darkness". . . . . "Lest ye utter by the tongue words easy to be understood how shall it be known what is spoken? . . . . For if I know not the meaning of the voice I am unto him that speaketh a barbarian and he that speaketh shall be a barbarian unto me. . . . ." Both Jesus Christ and St. Paul are clear about the need for a man to understand his own perceptions and his own utterances; in modern jargon we describe these as the terminal points of his communication system and modern management research and analysis adequately confirms the importance of subjective influences. When Jesus Christ counselled a man to remove the beam from his own eye before helping to remove the mote from his brother's, or advised the physician first to heal himself, He was speaking to all managers in all ages. It has been shown by modern quantitative methods that the manager who is significantly aware of his dependence upon his subordinates also produces a significantly superior performance.

Morale

The normal person seeks two satisfactions: security and self-expression. Since, in a modern economy, a man's employment is the most important influence that bears upon him, it is desirable to ask in what terms security and self-expression can be expected to appear. Security involves not only wages; it involves dependability or at least intelligibility in the work situation; beyond a threshold the unexpected and the random can be disturbing. On the other hand the complete determination of a man's work, as on certain assembly lines, giving him no discretion, no opportunity for solving problems on his own initiative, can be no less disturbing. There is some intermediate level at which the amount of unpredictability in a man's work is balanced by his need for self-expression, and at this level his adjustment to the work situation and those with whom he shares it will be effective; the morale of the enterprise, if others share his experience, is said to be high. Men have a broad expectation of what may happen, coupled with scope to use their initiative either in helping it to happen in accordance with some intelligible and collective plan, or else to correct things that go wrong. The essence of morale is a blend of reasonable intelligibility and effective initiative. Both of these demand close communication not only between those who make policy and those who implement it, between manager and workman, but also between workmen engaged on different aspects of the whole task. It can be shown that lateral communications, both in hospitals and coalmines, have a profound effect upon both morale and the effectiveness with which the task is carried out.

In enterprises subjected to the pressures of change or emergency the importance of free information flow, whether affecting goals, problems or resources, is paramount. If a senior manager does not have easy contacts with his immediate subordinates these cannot be on sensitive terms with their own colleagues or subordinates; a hospital matron not supported by her committee cannot support her nurses. The garment of truth is without seams; so likewise is the fabric of good management. Its indivisibility is the high quality of its communication system, and this quality is determined as much by the knowledge that the top management have of themselves as by the technical competence that they display to others. We live in a culture dominated by the need to be personally successful; any manager may be subjected to the sinister pressures of an ambitious family no less than to the organised drives of everyday commerce; the most self-respecting of men may yield under the double thrust, and seek relief in trying to pass himself off as somebody he is not; he may join this group or that, link his fortunes with this faction or the other, and choose for his family a style of life old and familiar, or new and uncomfortable; some will succeed more than others in the great game of OneUpManShip. But for each the same advice is needed: Whatever happens to all other channels of communication, try to keep free those by which one's inner motives, doubtful though they are known to be, at least can be observed. It is a handicap to any gambler that others should be able to read his cards more clearly than he can himself.

SCIENCE AND THE MANAGER

1. The Nature of Scientific Method

Consider the following: "A family of elephants, Father, Mother and Baby Jumbo, have sliding races one Sunday afternoon down a grassy hillside. Father, simply because he is heaviest, always wins, Mother always comes second, and Baby Jumbo, being lightest, always comes last, no matter how hard he tries."

This story will, no doubt, have different effects upon different readers; the Englishman, for example, will wish to know whether the elephants had any legal right to be on the hillside or whether they were causing damage to property; the Scot will protest about such behaviour upon the Sabbath; the Welshman will object to the unfairness of a competition in which the little is matched so unequally against the big. But there might be one reader to point out that, although it is not impossible to get elephants to slide down grassy hillsides, it would be highly unlikely that victory always went to the same beast. For it is nearly three hundred years since Galileo, the father of dynamics, first showed us that bodies do not descend under gravity at a speed proportional to their weight; this was a simple but erroneous doctrine drawn, like many other beliefs inherited from antiquity, from the untested assertions of Aristotle. The observable* fact is that the speed at which elephants slide down grassy slopes (when not deliberately impeding their descent by, say, digging their tusks into the ground) does not bear any predictable relation to their weight. A heavy one may, for a variety of reasons, come to a stop on the very surface that a less massive one glides gracefully across. While Galileo's experimental controversion of Aristotle's dogma does not consider sliding friction, which, especially with elephants, is a most complex subject, it justified new methods of exploring the secrets around us; our knowledge of the physical world is, in consequence, so extensive that some men are able to live their lives absorbed in one small corner of it. This knowledge is the foundation of modern technology, and there are two roots from which it has grown: first, our search for knowledge begins with the observation of Nature herself, and not with what we imagine Nature ought to be; we now find out at first hand what elephants (or electrons or planets) actually do instead of going by what we imagine they ought to do; second, the information we collect thereby is not only classified, but, as far as possible, measured. The gateways to modern science have painted over them the words "Facts and Figures". When we have grasped this, we do not make errors about which elephant wins most sliding races.

2. Management and Measurement

There are no doubt many managers, as well as scientists, for whom the claim of facts and figures is nothing new. They may, on the contrary, protest at being too much concerned with collecting and interpreting them already, and read with approval of how Marks and Spencer simplified their record system to dispense with tons of paper. Every shopkeeper will, for example, have long had some way of knowing what sales his assistants

---

*Some readers may find it inconvenient to carry out this experiment. It may be simulated by arranging two or three smooth boards, end to end, forming a slope of about 15°. It will be found that a wooden tray that will just slide down this slope when empty does not necessarily go faster when heavily loaded. It may even refuse to slide.

are making, and he will from time to time check what cash they have taken; the foreman on the building site will count how many bricks or slates or steel windows he has been using, and on what parts of the building; the manager of the coalmine will know how many miners have come to work, what sections of the mine they have gone into, and how many tons of coal they have filled at the end of two hours. All these, and a thousand other ways to collect and to use information, are among the activities of managers across the world, and no doubt similar numerical records were kept by those who built the Pyramids or the City of Rome. Even in the parable of the elephants the number and their rank order by weight are both exactly known.

It is thus legitimate to doubt whether there can be anything unfamiliar in the use of quantitative methods in management; some who, for example, deny that operational research offers the manager anything new may suggest that, had their grand-fathers not kept accurate and informative accounts, they could not have survived in business. And even the Ancient World had measurement, with elaborate systems of counting and of selling slaves; of allocating and collecting taxes; of provisioning armies, and even of arranging the elections of Emperors; all of these were carried to a high degree of arithmetical perfection. But it does not follow that numeration is necessarily the prelude to analysis; a man may count without drawing fresh conclusions from his results. Although information takes on order when measured, this alone does not guarantee insight or even under-standing. Over and above, therefore, our primary quest, for Facts and Figures, for observing and measuring, we must establish relationships between what we observe and measure if we are to progress in the sense of being scientific, or helping to establish a science.

A simple but far-reaching illustration of this is to be found in Newton's demonstration that the force pulling the apple to the ground in his Woolsthorpe orchard was also the force keeping the moon in its orbit overhead. The observable and measurable facts of the moon's rotation and of the fall of the apple had long been known, but it was Newton's insight, displayed in the suggestion that the two known effects were products of the same cause that made our knowledge of them taken together immensely more valuable than our knowledge of them taken separately. The ability to establish numerical relationships of this kind is to be compared with the power to arrange words into thoughts; every word in Goethe is to be found in a dictionary, but the new relationships into which he places them create ideas that will last as long as the German (and any other) language is spoken. It may well be that, at a practical level, management has long had an understanding of relationships not obvious from the recorded facts alone, even if this understanding has occasionally fallen short of Newton's. For example, that great pioneer of management practice, Wilkins Micawber, still at the close of a century the untarnished inspiration of so many of his fellow-countrymen, declared, "Annual income twenty pounds, annual expenditure nineteen, nineteen, six, result happiness. Annual income twenty pounds, annual expenditure twenty pounds ought and six, result misery"; and in this he illustrates a truth. But his eloquent numerical argument is merely to keep out of debt. He does not suggest any law to relate the magnitudes of debt and of misery, as the relationships discovered by Newton enabled him to forecast eclipses of the sun and moon, and to explain other celestial phenomena that had defied previous enquiry. Mr. Micawber is simply illustrating the experience of others with figures that tell us nothing new; it is his laconic mode of expression that we remember. And, partly because his maxim is so simple, partly because most managers will, by middle life, tend to agree with him, he is authoritatively quoted.

3. New Fields for Measurement

But let us regard the need for managers to grasp concepts more difficult than those of simple profit or loss; consider, for example, some of the human interactions upon which the arithmetic of profit and loss finally depends. Much industrial trouble, it is said, can be traced to failures of communication between different levels of the enterprise. . . . "If only people here could see where their behaviour is going to land us all. . . ." But not only do the directors express astonishment at the lightning strike, or the workpeople show alarm to read in their newspapers that, on the stroke of the previous midnight, their livelihoods have been sold to another firm previously held up as an immoral and remorseless competitor; there are confusion and obscurities at every moment of the day. In spite of this, if an outside observer asks any level of management how much it knows of what goes on below it, and what are the problems tormenting its subordinates, the answer is probably to suggest that these problems are well enough understood; it is not in knowing the problems but in securing the resources to solve them that the management task would be held to lie. It is thus of interest to apply to this field of knowledge our two criteria of observation and measurement.

The first example is drawn from the hospital field; all but one of forty matrons believed that they fully understood their ward sisters' problems, the one exception being a matron recently appointed. Of the six hundred ward sisters who served in their hospitals, 54% believed that their matrons were no longer in touch with these problems. The figures for industry are no less telling.

Of the shop floor operatives 28% believed that their own foremen understood the operatives' problems;

of these same foremen 88% believed they understood the problems of their own operatives;

of these foremen 43% believed that their own works' managers understood the foremen's problems;

of these works' managers 94% believed that they understood the problems of their own foremen;

of these works' managers 59% believed that their own general managers understood the problems of the works' managers.

Since most general managers believe they understand the problems of their own works, a rough managerial estimate of the transparency of the enterprise is 100 % x 94 % x 88 %, or, say, 83 %; this is the degree to which top management feel they understand the problems at the point of operation. Those who look upwards for understanding find their vision, however, more opaque; to them the measure of top management awareness is 28 % x 43 % x 59 % or, say, 7 %. To those below, an average of 7 % of their trouble will seem to be known, or understood, by the man at the top. This is a figure very different from 83 %; whatever objections may be raised against the methods used to get the information, that is, about the way in which the samples were chosen or the manner in which the interviews were conducted, it is clear that the management of this concern like the matrons of the hospitals, might, given such figures, well wish to question the efficacy of their communication systems.

A further illustration of measurement in this field reveals the views of shop stewards on problems of industrial discipline; there can hardly be any argument that these problems and the part of shop stewards in them are regarded by the public as well as by management as one of the most pregnant sources of inefficiency in the whole of British industry. But a random sample of 149 shop stewards, drawn from all over the country, replied to the remark:

"Workers can get justice only if disciplinary cases are decided by a committee on which workers are also represented"

with these opinions:

Strongly agree	37	Strongly disagree	15
Agree	31	Disagree	57
	Uncertain 9		

and to the remark:

"No matter who decides disciplinary cases, workers can get justice if the shop stewards are allowed to go up and discuss a case with the higher levels of management."

with these opinions:

Strongly agree	70	Strongly disagree	4
Agree	55	Disagree	14
	Uncertain 6		

The importance of these figures is not what some regard as the surprising confidence shown by the shop stewards in the fairness of their top managers, because measures of opinion are not in themselves surprising; they are simply numerical facts. The surprise is an emotion of the manager whose views are not supported by observational evidence collected by outsiders to whom his personal opinions are not relevant. This does not mean that, in the industrial situation, these same opinions are also irrelevant; they may, on the contrary, have the most calamitous consequences, such as holding up the construction of a liner for six weeks or throwing a whole assembly line idle. but this, too, is in the end a matter of factual observation. We must acknowledge, like the astronomer at an eclipse of the sun, that human beings may be blind to what is inconvenient, that they may actively oppose researches inviting them to change their opinions, or that they may subscribe to new opinions without in truth discarding the "wrong" ones they have long held. There is no guarantee that numerical evidence of human opinion different from one's own ever, of itself, led to an individual conversion, but it should help those, such as managers, to whom the views of others might be important, to have some estimate of how strongly those views are held.

However this may be, the connection between the results of these two studies cannot escape even those to whom simple arithmetic is an unfathomable mystery. In the first we find that the men on the shop floor feel that the chance of top management understanding their problems is about 7 %; in the second we find that 83 % of shop stewards believe that they will get justice if they can discuss their cases with top management personally. The two studies were independently conducted in different countries; both point to the need for understanding better how ideas are transmitted through systems of authority.

4. Management and the Electronic Computer

The diffusion of scientific method, from the research laboratory, from metals and fuels, electrons and atoms, to the Board Room, to problems of investment and markets, prices and exports, has coincided with the rise of the electronic computer. These two growths are indirectly related; some, but by no means all, of the management techniques that science has developed depend upon our ability to carry out long and repetitious exercises in arithmetic. But methods of observation, measurement and analysis can often be applied to the problems of the manager, as well as to those of the scientist, without the managers necessarily having access to the computer; and there is a real danger that simple and effective solutions of management problems will be overlooked because of the mistaken impression that they demand these sophisticated devices.

Nor is this all. For no computer programme has yet been designed automatically to identify management problems as such nor to write the programmes of instructions needed to solve them; the human operator, guided by his own sense of values, must both select the problem to be treated and specify the conditions of its treatment. Only then may he ask what help, if any, the computer has to offer; if he is fortunate he may discover that he can address to the machine both the facts and his instructions for their analysis. Only then may he assign to it the labour of computation, as a powered saw saves the muscles of the joiner in cutting the shapes that he desires. But the joiner alone decides what the saw is to do and how it shall be done, however much his choice of cut may, in the first place, be influenced by the design and power of the saws at his disposal.

The high speeds and capacities of modern computers enable managers to consider, in making up their minds, influences too complex to evaluate in a reasonable time by traditional methods. Such might be presented by the task of replacing a piece of plant or machinery at given interest rates, and when future operating and maintenance costs could be estimated for different levels of output. Of a number of different pieces of plant that would equally suit the technical operating needs, which would be the most satisfactory to select, supposing that capital costs, as well as capacities, maintenance and running costs, differed

among themselves? And if the decision were likely to recur at
short intervals, as with an electricity board continuously replacing its power stations or a transport undertaking its buses, with
constant rises in consumer demand and capital costs but constant improvements in maintenance and operating costs, how
would the decision be taken? For each new unit is then to take
its place among a mixture of various ages, and since the older
ones are used for fewer hours a day than the newer ones, and
since the present efficiency of the older ones depends not only
upon their previous use but also upon their maintenance record,
the search for the most economical policy becomes impossible
without an electronic slave to cleave our way through the jungles
of arithmetic. If, for example, the decline in operating efficiency
varies inversely as the annual expenditure on maintenance, how
should one's financial resources best be divided between new
capital plant and maintenance policy? With the growth of
highly capitalised industry these are not academic questions,
although they may demand the collection and analysis of
numerical data of an order of complexity normally to be found
only in research laboratories.

The use of computers to perform tedious routines, like the
payment of armies or the control of supplies, that have been
carried out by scribes since the days of Chaldea, are no more
than the extension, into the 20th Century, of methods that
began with a notch cut in a tally stick and are already known to
modern managers by their use of punched cards and electric
tabulators. The use of the machines for such work is clearly
enough the application of science to the problems of management, but so is carrying coal in the staterooms of the Queen
Elizabeth its application to the problems of transport; the
misapplication of these wonderful machines to clerical slavery
may be no less uneconomic than the manufacture of water from
pure hydrogen and oxygen.

5. Management, Randomness and Time

It is a frequent objection, by managers, to the use of quantitative methods that they never know what is going to happen next, or that all cases are different. Events can be so unrelated that they are said to occur at random, like the arrival times of planes at an airport, ships at a busy oil refinery or ambulances at a hospital. Sometimes disorder masks an underlying design, as in the arrival times of trains in a station, the weekly tonnages of coal produced at a pit, the number of pints of milk sold from day to day on a particular round, or the lengths of time that successive patients remain in a particular hospital ward. But such variations, whether complete disorder, as in random arrivals, or a mildly disarranged regular pattern, need not put us off. If one is able to discover, by the simple processes of observation and measurement, what particular pattern or degree of variation the events appear to follow, one can accept it as *an observed fact of the situation*. It is a victory of the quantitative method to describe these patterns of variation, *including complete randomness or disorder*, in a language that can both communicate ideas and form decisions. Since time began, management has recognised as its inescapable enemies the unexpected, the inaccurate, the untidy and the unpunctual. But over the past generation scientific methods have been evolved for analysing uncertainty, and, at times, for assigning its causes. And even in cases where causes are still untraceable, the effects of uncertainty can be allowed for in setting up the best managerial system, just as the engineer can allow, in designing and constructing a machine, for the possible failure of one of its parts. Perhaps that use of quantitative methods most profitable to management in the long run will be to aid the design and control of continuous processes subject to breakdowns, delays, interruptions and other real faults and variations beyond the power of management wholly to cure.

The general name for this quantitative method is Simulation. Just as traditional language can be used to describe a series of events as to suggest to an informed listener either what the outcome of those events might be, or what additional information he needs to seek that possible outcome, so also may the quantitative description of another train of events suggest either the quantitative outcome of those events, or the nature of the additional quantitative facts needed to suggest it. The use of measurement gives precision to the general question: "If when I do this and that, I find that the other tends to happen, what will be the result of doing, not this-and-that, but so-and-so? Or of doing neither this-and-that nor so-and-so, but such-and-such?" More formally this can be stated, "Given conditions P, Q, R, S, etc. . . . . . ., I find by observation that the result is X. What is likely to be the result if the conditions are changed to P^1, Q^1, R^1, S^1, ...?"

This kind of conumdrum is no doubt familiar to us from the primary school. "If I buy 10 eggs and 5 apples I find I must pay 4 shillings for them. What additional facts do I need to get the cost of 14 eggs and 17 apples?" From such illustrations we can develop plausible descriptions of managerial problems far too complex to be resolved by traditional mathematical analysis. For in the real world the prices of services or raw materials may fluctuate with the state of the market, the quantities needed may depend upon the capacity of the factory to take on more work, and the length of time to complete the next order may vary from 24 hours to 6 months. Nevertheless, given, *as an observational fact of the situation the manager is called upon to handle*, the pattern of variation among these quantities, he can frequently decide what is the most economical system of operations to employ. He may then seek the most economical system supposing the observed pattern of variation itself to vary.

6. An Example of Simulation: Monte Carlo Methods

Consider the following: It is observed that the number of tankers waiting in the approaches to a refinery varies from zero up to ten. Averaged over all kinds of tankers, the cost of waiting time is £1000 per day per tanker. Quantitative information can be found upon the

(a) distribution of tankers by type (crude-oil in, ballast out;

refined product in, different refined product out; ballast in, refined out; etc.)

(b) distribution of tankers by time alongside, discharging or loading cargo, washing tanks, etc.;

(c) number of jetties and availability for particular needs, e.g. discharging ballast;

(d) distribution of tankers by depth of draught, and hence by ability to berth at different levels of tide;

(e) fluctuations in hours of darkness during which certain types of tanker are forbidden to move in river;

(f) forecast of throughput of refinery and of future fleet capacity;

(g) costs of building extra jetties, installing discharge plant of increased capacity, deepening river, lighting fairway for movement during darkness, etc.

Under present conditions the average waiting time per tanker is 34 hours and 800 tankers use the refinery every year. Hence the annual cost of waiting time is more than one million pounds. What, if any, is the maximum economy to be achieved, what changes in operating conditions are needed to achieve it, and what will the cost of those changes amount to? Such changes of operating conditions include the

(i) building of one or more additional jetties;

(ii) provision of ballast discharging mains or other services at jetties now lacking them;

(iii) systematic reduction of the average time alongside of tankers, either by work study, the re-equipment of existing jetties, or the re-deployment of the labour force;

(iv) reduction of the total throughput of the refinery by deflecting elsewhere tankers likely to need to wait more than a given length of time;

(v) exclusion from the jetties of all tankers appearing to use them uneconomically (e.g. to effect repairs, to wash tanks or to take on or discharge small quantities of cargo only);

(vi) illumination of the fairway, the use of radar and so forth, to make possible the movement of tankers during darkness;

(vii) dredging of the river to make possible the passage of tankers at any state of the tide;

(viii) or any combination of these.

Some of these elements readily admit of more than one level of change; the average length of time alongside, for example, at present about 50 hours, could be reduced at various costs in wages or equipment by 10 %, 20 % or even 30 %. But there is no virtue in paying for this beyond the point at which it costs more than the value of waiting time saved; nor is it economic to pay for reducing time alongside if the same sum spent on a new jetty, or dredging the river, or lighting the fairway, would reduce the average waiting time still more. The interrelations between the various possibilities open to the owners of the refinery are of indescribable complexity, and yet, by the use of a particular branch of Simulation, known as the Monte Carlo method, a practical answer to the problem as stated was found by a team of four workers within one month. The answers to incidental questions (such as the likelihood of four or more ships wishing simultaneously to pump ballast into a common ring main) posed during the study alone justified the cost of the exercise. Without the use of quantitative information and methods to handle it this problem, like most others involving sequences of random events, could have been treated by intuition alone; and, if practical experience in management teaches us anything, it is the treachery of intuition when trying to solve queueing problems.

7. Quantitative Methods and Problem Structure

The use of measurement in tackling management problems must inevitably invite the question "But what is to be measured?"; quantitative methods often introduce concepts not previously thought about. For example, as soon as the manager asks the analyst, "What is the 'best' stock level that I should hold?" he must first define what is meant by "best". In the relative ease of purchasing in a stable market the "best" level is that at which the sum of the risk of loss due to running out of stock plus the risk of loss due to the cost of surplus stock being unnecessarily held is as small as possible. The problem then involves three separate elements of cost:

(a) the ordering cost, to include the cost of tenders, of delivery, of acceptance sampling, of settling the account; it may include the cost of setting-up to make a new batch;

(b) the holding cost, including the interest on capital tied up, insurance, deterioration, obsolescence, wages of store-keepers, rent and security;

(c) the shortage or stock-out cost, that is, the loss to the enterprise by delay in production or disappointment to the customer by not having the stock available.

If the demand for parts or stock varies from week to week the pattern of this variation is another fact of the situation that should be known. Given these four pieces of information, or estimates of them based upon measured experience, the "best" stock is easily determined. It would be a valuable use of the time of accountants to collect the figures needed for the optimising calculations, because, in Great Britain, the cost of holding industrial stock can be estimated at 2% of our national income and, what is more, the level of industrial stocks has, since 1955, been rising much faster than productivity. There is, without doubt, scope for the quantitative review of our stock policies in terms of the concepts here used. The analysis becomes more complicated when the market price and the run-out cost are no longer constant; one can nevertheless, from a knowledge of the likely range of fluctuation drawn from past experience, still estimate, not perhaps the "best" value in the sense used above, but the "most likely best" value.

A further extension of such ideas of structure and measurement is in the field of value analysis. The manager with a proper sense of control will ask "Besides assuring myself that my money is spent honestly, how do I know whether I am getting greatest value for it?" Consider, for example, the auditor who for several years had sampled about 20,000 vouchers of a firm that dealt in stationery and office machinery: typewriters, calculating machines, staplers, ribbons and so forth. One day the profitability of the firm came under question and he discovered, by carrying through a train of analysis outside his normal duties, that on over 60 per cent of its transactions the firm was losing money. It is no defence in bankruptcy to say that one had been honest; an auditing system that accounts meticulously for every penny of expenditure but cannot foresee ruin is of no use in a competitive economy. For the true application of quantitative methods is not merely to ask "Are these measurements correct and do they tally?", but also to enquire "What are these measurements for in the first place?" It is this question that directs attention to the underlying logic of the task by which the manager is confronted. And when the underlying logic, or structure, of the problem has been seen, the manager may then well pause to ask why the problem arises and, indeed, what are the wider objectives that he is trying to fulfil. We must not, therefore, regard the quantitative or scientific method merely as giving a little precision to something we could already do by less precise methods; what begins with a search for detailed accuracy may end by transforming total strategy.

8. Conclusion

There are four forces bearing upon management today that encourage a new approach to its primary task of taking decisions. The first is the need for economy of managerial time and effort; the Victorian era of abundance, as it was thought to be, of abundant manpower, abundant food, abundant raw materials, abundant servants, has gone; the age of science that replaces it is one of economy, of prudent thought, precise design, exact calculation. Management cannot escape this haunting by the Zeitgeist; it must weigh its decisions with all the nicety of the laboratory physicist experimenting on the atomic nucleus.

The second, related to the first, is the entry into the management process of the analytical approach familiar for three centuries to the scientist; while intuition, or the unremembered urges of the past, must always be the first weapon of the manager, he must also be able to grasp the *underlying structure* of the situations that challenge him, and know of any new methods that may help him in modifying it.

Thirdly, in the past fifty years the study of variability, through the methods of statistics, has brought to the help of managers a language to describe the unexpected, the capricious and the random elements of their tasks; and, fourthly, the rise of the social sciences has thrown a little light upon the human forces that, in the final analysis, determine whether or not any enterprise will succeed.

In Europe, as in America and in Russia, these new ideas are transforming the nature of the manager's task, and it is essential that those in control of industrial and commercial policy should know what promise they may hold. Just as, for example, the technology of oil refining, or of electronics, is a highly specialised business of which industrial directors cannot be expected to grasp all the working details, so also is management science highly specialised in its turn. But of the scope and limitations of science all managers and policy makers should be aware; it is no longer the sufficient mark of a gentleman, even at Cambridge, to know the Cavendish as 'Stinks'.

A STUDY OF TECHNICAL KNOWLEDGE

Substance and Shadow

Industrial workers often regard theory as no more than a
silhouette of practice; it is *doing* the job that is the substance,
and the human intelligence, shining upon the solid reality of
things achieved, must, like the sun, cast a shadow of nothingness behind it. Indeed, if the industrialist sometimes agrees that
theory and practice are connected even to the extent of the substance and the shadow, he is nevertheless confident that the real
apparatus of the factory, the workers, the machines and the
clocks, can be set into motion without regard to the unsub-
stantial phantoms that chase one another through the imagination of the theorist. It is both said and believed that an ounce
of practice is better than a ton of theory: or, that a plan of
action, framed on scientific laws and observed premises, is
nothing like as valuable a guide to success as a good hunch
from a sound, practical man.

It is not merely the hard-headed few who take this line. The
belief permeates all levels of industry, and all sections of it; the
imagined contrast between knowing and doing stands out like
the pattern of a chess board. We have, on the one hand, the
men whose contacts are with things: the labourer, the fitter, the

foreman, the engineer, all priding themselves on being practical men. On the other hand are the draughtsmen, the clerks, the accountants and the planners, who think themselves rather above the others, and who are not disinclined at times to talk disparagingly, or even offensively, about nuts-and-bolts men. One sees it also in academic circles; the professor of ecclesiastical history ridicules the endowment, at an ancient university, of an institute of agricultural research; the professor of aeronautics deplores spending great sums of money on the purchase of early printed books. There is no hatred so deep as for a scholarship one does not share. But the contrasting attitudes in industry, between desk and bench, plan and execution, are less excusable. Thought and action are, more often than not, in subdued conflict; the ultimate value to industry of a new idea can frequently be gauged by the derision with which it is first saluted—such, as, for example, the proposal that, before spending time and money upon schemes for education in management, it would be useful to conduct researches into the nature of management. This opposition is not, as might be thought, always a product of insecurity; it is often an honest belief that decision-taking processes do not lend themselves to objective study. These are essentially "practical" things done by busy men, and do not conform to "theoretical" ideas.

The Illusion of Pure Practice

There are undoubtedly senses in which practical knowledge can be said to exist, untramelled by the abstractions of academic science, unrelated, in the mind of its users, to any transcendental principle. A man may be taught to extract square roots on a slide rule, without ever having heard of logarithms, still less of indices or the exponential series. But we must not say he has no ideas about "theory". He has. He does not pick the instrument up blindly, and after a spasm of uncontrolled finger movements tell the answer. He does not act at random, as Thomas Huxley suggested the monkeys might, strumming upon the typewriters until they produced the Bible. He has preconceptions of what to do. He follows a drill that has been laid down for him, and to this extent he works in accordance with a theory. So does every practical man; the crossing sweeper knows, and knows as soon and he sets to work, how to do the job with the least effort; he knows, and can turn to good use, the compass of his sweep, the gathering power of his broom, the flow of the liquid mud, and so forth; he neither lays about him anyhow, a bit here and a bit there, sweeping the same mud twice over the same spot, nor does he go to the job in a blind fury; he does not sit down and wait for the intervention of a miraculous providence. Like the slide rule operator, he has a theory; he thinks ahead about what to do. And this thought is a necessary preparation for future action, like loading a gun before firing it. He thinks first, in accordance with his theory, and acts afterwards, thereby revealing to the world both his practice and his theory. Hence a grasp of theory is to some extent the ability to take preparatory action, and practice cannot successfully be carried through without it, unless by pure chance, like the widow who wins on the treble chance and knows nothing of football.

Doubt and Security

Some may feel it goes deeper than this. Human beings would hardly have grouped themselves into two parties if there were no more in the supposed contrast than mere definition. It is not just for this, we feel, that theorists and practitioners waste so much time disputing their relative importance, sometimes speaking of the others in terms of real abuse. The very words "a practical man" can even imply disparagement in terms of social class. In France there is a word of contempt for elaborate written plans—"paperasserie". A man was prosecuted in America for calling another an egghead; when an intelligent man disagrees with the popular press in Britain he is called highbrow or long haired. An explanation of this divergence is given by John Dewey in his Gifford Lectures for 1929, published as *The Quest for Certainty*. He argues that mankind, in perpetually seeking shelter and security amid the alarms and perils of this world, has striven always to know and to worship the enduring and immutable law behind the accidental and uncertain panorama of every-day life. Theory has become associated with the former, with the enduring truths, with the perfect and the transcendental. Practice has been manifest in the latter, in the vicissitudes of fate, in death, famine, pestilence, flood, earthquake and thunderbolt; in the luck of the harvest and of the mine; in all the uncertainties of life as it is lived. And hence theory and practice have come to be paired off as Heaven and Earth; the soul and the body; the spirit and the flesh; the serene, perfect and eternal as opposed to the violent, transitory and profane. Dewey regrets our construction of this contrast in the following words:

"The thing which concerns all of us as human beings is precisely the greatest attainable security of values in concrete existence. The thought, that the values which are unstable and wavering in the world in which we live are eternally secure in a higher realm (which reason demonstrates but which we cannot experience) . . . may give consolation to the depressed. But it does not change the existential situation in the least. The separation, that has been instituted between theory and practice . . . has had the effect of distracting attention and diverting energy from a task whose performance would yield definite results".

There may be two additional reasons that, as human experience accumulated and began to fall into or suggest recognisable patterns, led men to rate the theoretical and transcendental above the practical and concrete. Firstly, the accidents of every-day life were, as time went on, gradually recognised to be but ordinary events of which the full causes were not known or could not be foreseen. The collapse of the cathedral spire was no longer regarded as a pure accident; it was not still seen as a deliberate act of God. It was the result of insufficient regard for the laws of statics, and as these became better known and more rigorously observed, so the accidents became fewer. Likewise, it was not fate, nor evil spirits, that turned the milk sour; simple regard for cleanliness triumphed over the seemingly capricious. Hence men must have become impressed with the control that theoretical or abstract knowledge could exercise over practical events; idolatrous worship of the secret writing that gave men power is one of the earliest of all recorded human weaknesses. Secondly, it must have been observed at a very early stage that the number of men able to employ theoretical constructs was smaller than of those able to command the visibly practical affairs. For example, the geometers of Egypt, who could calcu late how to divide out the land, compared with the number who could dig it when it had been divided, must have been few, even within a privileged class structure. For primitive practice demands only the power of miming the visible operations; to see the spade as a spade, and to imitate the actions of another man in detail—even to the rituals of corn planting, the sacrifices made during its growth, the dances at the harvest, and any other functional pageantry. In contrast, the command of theoretical operations implies the ability to remember a code and to interpret it in the differing circumstances of practice. How far "abstraction" is an ability additional to and beyond "imitation" is no doubt a difficult question in semantics and psychology, but it is still a fact of modern industrial training that fewer men can be taught, and can apply in changing con- ditions, a set of self-consistent principles, such as the theory of alternating current, than can repeat the visible operations of some traditional craft, such as the winding of standard arma- tures. It is a matter of degree; the man who copies the action of the master bricklayer in laying on the mortar with his trowel is perhaps doing something merely simpler in degree than the foreman who controls the mixing of the mortar, or the clerk of works who agrees the setting out of the wall. Yet it is a fact that many men can be taught to use trowels, while few can be taught to use theodolites. Hence the more remote the know- ledge from the action of the hands upon the tools, the greater the mystery that envelops it, since it appears to be the province of the few.

Knowing by Doing

The doctrine that "Knowledge is Power" can be traced before the day of Francis Bacon. He writes of his philosophy:—

"The matter in hand is no mere felicity of speculation, but the real business and fortunes of the human race, and all power of operation. For man is but the servant and interpreter of nature; what he does and what he knows is only what he has observed of nature's order in fact or in thought; beyond this he knows nothing and can do nothing. For the chain of causes cannot by any force be loosed or broken, nor can nature be commanded except by being obeyed. And so those twin objects, human knowledge and human power, do really meet in one; and it is from ignorance of causes that operation fails".

We have already seen that theory is sometimes "preparatory action"; it is getting ready to do something. But many people in order to do something need to be confronted with the situation in which they have to do it. The billiard player needs to have his cue poised over the table to work out his next stroke, analysing with the sensation of his arms and shoulders the dynamics of the table as he could not analyse them with pencil and paper; the batsman thinks, in the moment before striking the ball, with his muscles and his bat, not in terms of the abstract concepts of particle dynamics; the stone mason and the sculptor design and figure with their mallets and chisels as they go along; even the lawyer, drawing up a complicated contract, must allow the pen to form his ideas for him as it runs over the paper. And, at a much less specialised level, there are many people, old as well as young, who must hold audible conversations with themselves to decide upon their next move.

Dewey insists that, in this context, activity and the analysis of that same activity are identical. This supports the theory of

J. B. S. Watson that thought is no more than a delicate and highly complex, if generally imperceptable, working of the physical organs, the lips, vocal chords and even the grosser muscles. The crowd at the athletic meeting runs every stride at the victor's shoulder; their hearts and their breathing quicken as his quicken. The violinist understands the behaviour of stretched strings, not in terms of algebra and physics, expressing relations between length, tension, linear density and pitch, but in terms of technical execution, of where the fingers are placed and how the bow is drawn, of how the strings are tuned; when he sees a note on the paper he does not say "an oscillation of 440 periods a second, with a long train of harmonics, etc.", he knows it by the name of "A", because he has been told that others call it that for identification. But above all he knows it as a sound produced on his violin, and responds to it, even if only in imagination, with his fingers at the appropriate place on the instrument. And if somebody starts talking to him about musical theory, about pitches and intervals, he will follow the argument, either with his fingers moving in imagination on an imaginary violin, by seeing the notes on an imaginary score, or by hearing them in his head. He does not think abstractly, of simple harmonic motion, energy transmission and so forth. He goes through an imaginary performance. He acts inside his mind, and his action is his theory. In other words, like any other person, he tries to understand the situation in terms with which he is already familiar, namely, of playing a fiddle.

To John Dewey, therefore, knowledge has one facet only; it cannot be called either practical or theoretical; knowledge is merely that fund of human ability that enables men to control their environment, or if not to control it, for one would not pretend to control the Aurora Borealis or the weather, then to make use of it. One uses a knowledge of the weather for aircraft navigation or for agriculture; a knowledge of the Northern Lights helps us to understand the weather or to improve radio transmission around the world, or to account for the changing orbit of the Russian satellites. For Dewey our knowledge of, say, the strength of materials is merely our capacity to build railway bridges or colliery winding gear that will stand up to the strain of their work. There is, according to Dewey, no meaning in abstract generalities; what others would call theorising, or trying to pull to pieces a situation to see of what factors it is composed, so that one may understand the situation, is, to Dewey, actually commanding it. One does not, in fact, "understand" or "interpret" things; one actually deals with them, makes use of them, and hence alters them.

Dewey's elevation of practice to the same level as theory has had an important reflection in American life. To deny that there is any moral distinction between knowing and doing, between the transcendental and the experiential, between thought and action, has glorified the practical and mechanic activities of the world. Heaven is no longer in a supernatural realm. It is here and now, making material things, using them to increase the clatter of earthly strife and distraction. Amassing money, being busy, "getting on with the job", are all at least the equal of thought and contemplation; vigorous action replaces philosophical reflection; "Come on, let's go" is the stereotype of American films. It is the possession of material things that glorifies the Lord; in this pragmatic philosophy lies the justification of the fortune seeker and the man of business. In its less defensible forms it appears as Henry Ford's "What is commercially right is morally right"; in the endless elaboration of means without regard to the values of the ends they serve—the long journeys made in powerful and luxurious cars for the sole purpose of returning home again; in the life of the greatest man of action of them all—the gangster.

For all this, famous men describe themselves in *Who's Who* as professors of *theoretical* physics; humble men hang signs in their windows calling themselves *practical* chimney sweeps. But there is no pure, ideal, perfect, absolute and transcendental body of knowledge, uncontaminated by human experience, that can be called "theoretical" physics, if "theoretical" is taken to mean "intuitively revealed"; the Greeks made the mistake of thinking that there was, and invented the Never-Never Lands in which such perfections might exist. They tried to formulate the laws of Nature without regard to their own experience of the world of Nature, or, as we should say, without regard to the facts. They taught that bodies fall at a speed proportional to their weight, and it was nearly two thousand years before Galileo (it is said) dropped different weights, to fall at the same speed, from the leaning tower of Pisa. Likewise with the self-styled practical chimney sweep; he may know little of the aerodynamics, as such, of vertical columns of air, and still less of the mathematics of particle diffusion, but unless he works in accordance with a preconceived plan, and incorporates sound ideas about setting out his dust sheets, and restricting the drift of his soot, observing a plan valid in theory as well as adroit in execution, he is unlikely to keep many customers for long. It is possible, no doubt, to be an excellent car driver without ever having seen what lies beneath the bonnet; one need know nothing of the theory of the internal combustion engine nor of the transmission of power. This may well be so, since neither of those has to do with the purely manual operations of driving. On the other hand, it will be a poor driver who has not learned, whether by having accidents or by avoiding them, that certain laws of friction can be discerned in the behaviour of cars on wet roads or steep hills; or that turning corners quickly and taking hump-backed bridges at speed tend to make a car leave the road. These experiences incorporate some of the theoretical ideas needed to be understood by good drivers, and nobody would get very far, in any campaign to ensure safety on the Queen's Highway, by asserting that there was no need for the practical motorist to worry about them. One does not drive a car about on the assumption that the laws of friction and of centrifugal force are different from what they are, nor, even that, being purely theoretical, one can act in defiance of them.

Ordered Knowledge not necessarily mathematical

It is clear that theoretical knowledge need not necessarily be set down in mathematical terms. In practice it is helpful if it can be, as mathematics is universal, and can be read by many people. In engineering, operational processes are usually expressed in terms of mathematics, because their control demands exactitude, the right temperature, the right mixture, the right voltage and so forth. To persuade Nature to make for us what we want her to make, we must design numerical scales to be sure that our quantities and conditions are as they should be. But there are other activities demanding high accuracy for which we do not dress our theory up in formal mathematical garb. Music provides an example. One of the most exacting collective technical operations known to men is the performance of an orchestral symphony. And though to perform in the Albert Hall one may need no understanding of the philosophical nature of time, nor of the psychological reasons for one key being melancholy and another cheerful, it is important that the conductor understands with great precision the highly intricate formalities of the score. An understanding which merely enables one to talk about the symphony during the interval is not a conductor's understanding; that lies in the performance and in the performance alone. Any other understanding is useful for practical conversation, but it cannot pretend to be a theoretical knowledge of what the conductor does on the rostrum.

It is of interest to trace the antecedents of Dewey's "higher realm which reason demonstrates but which we cannot experience", that has seized the imagination of men, and been held by them as the eternal and the perfect. A second concept of this world, a new code of immutable law, has evolved in the last few centuries as the compact structure of modern science; for it is a perfection both rational and objective and quite different from the Fairyland of Wishfulness that is the refuge of failure and frustration. To those of us who deal with material things, with coalcutters, cogging mills and spinning frames, the perfect world I am trying to describe is the one in which mathematical tables and scientific methods are always and exactly true, that perfect world compared with which the actual happenings in the mines and factories are only a series of irritating disappointments.

The Fantasy Stage

Human intelligence seems to master the secrets of Nature in three jumps. In the forgotten past, something unusual has caught the attention of some observant man, who marvels at the new effect. He has, sooner or later, sought to find out how it happened, so that he might repeat it and thereby astonish his friends. He would not be satisfied until he was able to reproduce it at will. The study of electricity started with elegant gentlemen in powdered wigs giving their friends electric shocks from Leyden Jars, or amusing themselves by making the legs of dead frogs kick again, or by drawing sparks from kite lines during thunder storms. Frederick the Great would order a regiment of grenadiers to clasp hands in a chain and amuse his companion buffoons by making them leap as one to the electric impulse. James Watt is, traditionally, supposed to have marvelled at the pressure of the steam in the kettle; coal itself was a mere curiosity, a black stone that burned; even the study of radio-activity, which in fifty years has transformed the world, started by making the physicists marvel exceedingly when Becquerel discovered that his wrapped photographic plates were fogged if left near uranium oxide. Certainly its first impact on the popular imagination was as magic, and the marvels of the contemporary discovery of X-rays are preserved in their very name. This first and exciting acquaintance with a new phenomenon may be called the "fantasy stage". The fields of pure metals and of long chain molecules are fuller of fantasies than the whole of classical mythology. This stage, both in the emotions that it evokes, and by its lack of sophistication, may be compared to human infancy.

The Profit Stage

Once the control of the new effect has been secured, even if only partially, but still before it has been explained in terms of what is already known, there are those who seek its use. For to them, and they form the majority of this world, nothing is of interest unless something can be done with it. An unknown lady is supposed to have asked Faraday what was the value of his new discovery of electromagnetic induction, and to have been answered with the question, "Madam, of what use is a newly born baby?" Anybody who has worked in a research laboratory will know that the first question from the lay visitor is invariably "But what's it all for?" Any answer about knowledge for its own sake is received with scepticism and disappointment; the layman likes to persuade himself that the research worker is about to announce something such as how to turn lead into gold, the elixir of life, perpetual motion, or three-dimensional coloured television sets, from which life-sized actresses emerge and offer to embrace him. It is use, not knowledge, that is next demanded after the fantasy stage.

So these early tricks with electricity and steam were harnessed by ingenious inventors; the telegraph and telephone, even the Atlantic cable, were working, usefully if not perfectly, before the laws of transmission of alternating currents down inductive circuits were known; the Great Eastern had finished her work of laying the first cable before Lord Kelvin had solved his famous equations; the steam engine had evolved almost to its modern form before the science of thermodynamics had become unified; in radioactivity, the atomic bomb has been made to work before there is any final theory of nuclear structure. In quite different fields, the violin family had already evolved their familiar shape two centuries at least before Lord Rayleigh mathematically demonstrated its perfection; Johann Kepler was trying to use the movements of the planets for something extremely useful when he stumbled across his famous laws: he was trying to cast horoscopes, and there could be nothing more useful than a reliable horoscope. Human nature being what it is, its next efforts after discovery, after the fantasy stage, are aimed at applying the novelty for use or profit; it is the industrial pioneer, seeking development and application, to whom the second stage truly belongs. It is convenient to call it then the "profit stage". This is, by and large, the great domain of industrial production and commercial enterprise, the real world of practice. In human terms, it represents adolescence, the age of utility, when action and achievement for their own sake hold the attention of vigorous immaturity, all motor bikes and transistor sets.

The Analysis Stage

As soon as the discovery is found to have useful application, it is desirable that it should be used effectively. It is therefore investigated, and as much as can be found out about it thereby related to what is already known. This phase of systematic analysis and synthesis necessarily comes third; research is pursued in order to find out what are the important factors in the "profit" aspects of the phenomenon, and which of these can be applied more cheaply or faster or made more industrially and commercially efficient. This is the function of industrial research; it is also largely the function of academic or so-called "pure" research, but not exclusively, because this is sometimes, as we have seen, involved in the "fantasy" stage. The formulation of general laws and the pursuit of knowledge in Dewey's "higher realm", whether that realm is canopied over the world of physics, chemistry, biology, history, language, psychology, or whatever it may be, normally follows the growth of the subject for its practical and utilitarian outcome. One striking result of the Russian satellite was the recognition in America that it had neglected its fundamental research programme; too much attention had been given to the utilitarian know-how, not enough to the analytical know-why. If the fantasy stage may be likened to human infancy, and the profit stage to adolescence, the analysis stage must represent the maturity of the adult. The essential mark of the fully grown mind is its desire to understand cause and effect.

Theory the Notation of Practice

In a short and crowded life, scientific theory has the great advantage of conciseness. A few simple laws can summarise generations of arduous practical experience; our command of steam power can be formalised and recorded in such a way that in a few lessons a student can grasp the underlying principles of it without needing to stumble through years of trial and error. In a hundred lessons, Macaulay's intelligent schoolboy can learn all the geometry discovered by the Egyptians in three thousand years of land surveying; he can be taught more chemistry in a week than Priestley discovered in his life-time. But he does so only because scientific theory, the expression of the third, or analytical stage, condenses into simple formulae the extremely mixed and confused consequences of practice and experiment. Theory may provide us with a key to open the gates of natural mystery, but it is a key that has been patiently forged by thousands of men in that furnace of adversity, failure and disappointment that we call practical experience. In the words of Karl Pearson, "Science provides the description in conceptual shorthand of the routine of our perceptual experience"; or of Leonardo de Vinci, "All true sciences are the result of experience that passes through our senses."

Rules of Thumb

The simple rules that the analysis stage distils from the "profit-stage" need not be mathematical in form. They can be the empirical drills, or codes of working practice, that are slowly evolved and tested in the light of experience. The laundress who spits on her iron need know little about the surface geometry of fluids. There is a vast field of knowledge, whose "theoretical" foundations are very shaky indeed if tested by the rigorous disciplines of physics or mathematics. Medical science is full of empirical rules of this kind. And industry does not reject empirical rules that cannot be "explained" in terms of pure science; it is quite satisfied to get its "know-how" into any systematic form that can be transmitted and relied upon. The engineer's manuals are filled with working rules, but it would puzzle many engineers to develop these rules from first principles. So when we talk about theory as the consistent recording of practice we do not necessarily mean in terms of fundamental science. This is a very important point and has great bearing on our systems of technical education. We must be content at times for the "analysis" stage to give us no more than a useful set of rules of thumb; if it tidies up the panorama of practical experience in terms of physics, chemistry, mathematics, or any of the other fundamental sciences we can explain our rules of thumb in terms of "scientific laws". Rules of thumb are more likely to be modified in the light of further experience than scientific laws, but they are still rules, even if different ones. It is in this sense that we have previously referred to the theories of the crossing sweeper and the chimney sweep. Their operating rules, neat, orderly, systematic, are all as much the fruits of experience and discipline, as are the laws of electromagnetic induction or statistical mechanics.

The Relation of Plan to Action

The division of labour is one of the most familiar features of modern industry. The assembly line has sub-divided the total task with a microscopic intensity; even before its appearance the tailoring trade provided striking illustrations of trying to multiply nothing by infinity. So it is not to be wondered at that one of the main divisions of a total task is between those who conceive and plan it, on the one hand, and those who perform the manual or physical operations that finally accomplish it on the other. *This division is not made because plans are said to be theoretical while execution is said to be practical.* It is made because most men have no time to learn more than one trade or profession, and, in the economy of Western civilisation, their working lives are thought to be most profitably spent if they become expert in one particular occupation alone. Hence industry employs those who make policy and those who carry it out; the designers and the producers; the draftsmen and the fitters; the architects and the builders. In other fields we find the politician and the general; the author and the publisher; the composer and the orchestra; when we see all these pairs we must not make the mistake of thinking that it is the "theory" men on the one hand against the "practical" men on the other. The division, in some activities at least, notably building, has been sharpened by commercial demands; the industrialist needing factories for his machinery and houses for his workers has tended to drive a wedge between the architect and the builder. Design has not infrequently become academic; construction seldom displays any features beyond those expedient in the saving of cost, and the trend is now to employ engineers rather than architects to design as well as to erect.

If there is a job, J, to be done which in this world of divided labour is best done by two men, let us say A and B, of whom A plans and B executes, then A and B are doing two quite different things, like two members of a relay team covering successive but different stages in the same race, or like the wife washing the dinner things before the husband dries them. If A's contribution is K and B's contribution is L, then J is equal to K plus L. This does not make K and L different aspects of the same thing, except in the sense that the numbers 5 and 7 can be said to be different aspects of 12. Nor can one say that K is purely theoretical, while L is purely practical. In the terms of this essay, K and L can, of course, be thought of as *each* having both theoretical and practical aspects. In this event J must be regarded as the sum of *four* terms, since K and L must now be duplicated in the mirrors of the mind. We do not normally envisage all of them; we fix swiftly upon what we call the designer's abstract idea, floating as a vapour in his consciousness, and upon the maker's visible manipulation of his tools and materials, all sweat and muscle. But the designer's *practice*, which consists in giving his thoughts visible form, such as preparing his working drawings, quantities and specifications, on the one hand, and the manufacturer's theory, on the other, or his planning, before he starts work, to marshall and apply his resources, do not so readily impress themselves upon us. Dewey would at once tell us that the second split, of K and L to make four terms, is meaningless; to Dewey the designer's abstract idea *is* the preparation of the working drawings, the bills and the specifications; to him the manufacturer's preparations and forward planning *are* essentially operations of physical production.

Technical Education

There are here consequences for education. If K has in fact no separable theoretical and practical aspects (and it is certainly not endowed with duality simply by being distinguishable from L in that different men can do each), it is idle to say that education aimed at teaching architect A how to do job K can be *either* theoretical *or* practical. Likewise with L; one cannot choose to give builder B either a theoretical or a practical education to learn L; nor can the education of either start with theory, and then go on to practice or *vice versa*. If K is a job done by one man, A, then A needs a knowledge of all the steps of that job, and, for those who care to think so, every one of these steps, whatever they may be, has both practical and theoretical aspects, since he both does it and is, in doing it, aware of what he is doing.

To fix our ideas, let us consider L, the task of B, the builder. It will demand a knowledge of how to read a drawing, how to lay bricks and how to set out a footing. But it is wrong to say that reading a drawing is theoretical while laying a brick is practical, or that considering levels in setting out footings is theoretical as opposed to the practical act of digging them. All parts of the task as equally to get the job done. There is no building "theory" as such that can be left out of B's educational course, if, say, he is pressed for time, and it is thought important not to sacrifice any of his "practical" work. One could, of course, decide not to teach B how to calculate the number of bricks in a wall of given dimensions, nor to estimate the weight of cement and sand needed to bond them. But this is not cutting back on theory to preserve time for practice; it is simply shortening the syllabus, just as leaving out all reference to the tasks of, say, laying tiles or hanging paper would also shorten it. It is impossible to teach any purely practical process or manual act that does not require thought or recognition of some kind; nor that does not demand some grasp of a system, code, order of work, or "theory"; teaching infants by numbers and rhymes, or low-grade recruits by words of command are examples. At a still lower level, sheep-dogs can be taught to respond to signals, and even to marshal their sheep in the most economical way. The dogs may have no need of theory, in the sense of understanding the properties of geodesics, but it would be difficult to deny that there is a difference between the trained and the untrained dog. Even if both come from the same litter, and are indistinguishable as they snooze in front of the cottage fire, one has an ability that is denied the other, and this ability is his theory.

It is the close relationship of K and L, the tasks of A the architect, and of B the builder, which causes the confusion. Because there is a sense in which A plans and B executes, in that B takes on where A leaves off, A is said to attend to the "theory" and B to the "practice" of their common task. But if we choose to think of the theoretical aspects of B's job, we see that they are not what A is doing. Nor are the practical aspects of A's job (as we may imagine them separately to exist) what B is doing. The theoretical part of building operations is not the job of the architect; nor is the practical part of the architect's task to put up the actual building. The architect must know enough about the builder's trade to design a house that is in fact buildable, but as the art of building advances it becomes possible to build a house to the same architectural design in a score of different ways. These many ways are no more the practical manifestations of the same theoretical master image than are twenty different ways of drying the same dinner service the practical reflections of one way of washing it.

Formal Representations of Achievement

It should help us to fix our ideas if we consider the following short table. This gives the distribution of the work involved in building a house, in both its paper and its operational stage; inside each of these stages are shown their theoretical and practical aspects. For simplification the planners have been lumped together, as have the manual workers concerned with the movement and manipulation of the physical materials.

Planning Stage

The task, K, of architect A (representing also any ventilation, heating, sanitary and other consultants advising upon any special services), is to produce all the drawings, bills and specifications necessary for job J.

(1) Theoretical Aspects of Planning Stage:
These include a clear image of the uses to which the building will be put at the price the owner is able to pay, the traditions and principles of architectural design, of structural science, of quantity surveying, of engineering and so forth.

(2) Practical Aspects of Planning Stage:
These include the physical preparation of the specifications, drawing and bills, specific to job J, with the assurance that, for example, the staircase will fit, that the roof will not blow away, nor the cisterns freeze at the first tough of abnormal weather, that the quantities specified in the bills will be both necessary and sufficient, and that these drawings, bills, and so forth will be ready on specified dates and convenient for use in whatever conditions they need to be used.

Production Stage

The task L, of builder B (representing also any ventilation, heating, sanitary and other contractors physically installing any special services) is to complete the total job J in accordance with the drawings, bills, and specifications that are the final products of task K. Like the relay runner, Builder B takes over from Architect A, just as A took over from Owner O, and as Owner O in turn took over from the circumstances, economic or emotional, that impressed upon him the need for a building.

(3) Theoretical Aspects of Production Stage:
These include the legends and the myths of the builder's trade in so far as these embody the cunning and the skill of the living craftsman; his codes of practice, his ideas upon the organisation and setting out of his work, his knowledge of what to do in abnormal weather, all, in fact, the accumulated lore of five thousand years; they include, or should include, ideas upon the collective tasks, that is, upon the division and programming of labour, upon the properly sequenced delivery of materials and the harmonious interlocking of the different tradesmen who work upon the same set of materials, or who knock holes in the same brick wall; they include ideas upon how to manage men in a casual trade paid at hourly rates or by specified tasks; indeed, they include ideas on all the myriad of relations that springs into existence as soon as the human and physical operations are set into motion.

(4) Practical Aspects of Production Stage:
These include the actual handling of the trowels and the mortar, the erection of the scaffolding, the connecting-up of the water supply, the sawing and hammering, and all the other visible and fascinating appearances of activity that the crowd lingers to admire. At the collective level they include the directions proper to job J given by the general foreman to decide in what particular order the various trades will follow one another in particular places on the job, and by the foreman bricklayer, for example, to his particular men upon their daily assignments.

Educational Implications

A study of the four sub-paragraphs repays our attention. We readily perceive the importance of the first and the last. What is an architect to us but a man versed in the traditions and glories of an art that has for centuries astonished the gaping pilgrims? What is a builder but a man with dust on his coat, a trowel in his hand, and a cloth cap on his head? Our national system of education is designed to turn our architects who respect the canonical styles, and builders who are good practical men with trowel or mallet. The accent has been either on "theoretical" planning or on purely manual "practice". But the total job has other aspects. The architect has to produce drawings that can, in fact, be used to work from. In practice, his office generally has a staff of juniors and assistants who can look after these, acting, as it were, on the architect's own fingers; the physical preparation of drawings and bills of quantities is usually too laborious for a busy architect himself to work at; he is driven to create through his assistants, and by verifying their finished work. So the meaning of the second sub-paragraph is really grasped; whether Stage (2) attracts the attention it deserves is another question.

The third, too, may tell a different story. It contains all the codes, systems, rules of thumb, "theoretical" ideas mirrored in the progress of the actual building operations on the site. It has nothing directly to do with the planning of the building: its cost, the amount and quality of the materials and so forth. These are already settled within the province of the planners, the architect and his team of surveyors and other specialists. But in the third sub-paragraph are all the ideas and systems, which, so to speak, the bricklayers mix with the mortar, with which the general foreman makes clear his orders to the leading tradesmen under him, which direct the eye of the carpenter as he rips his saw along the joists, and which even keep the tea-boys' account on the right side. It is the "know-how" of the Americans, the harvest of practical experience, shaped and ordered by economy and intelligence. Dewey would say that it is the capacity that all these men on the site need to do their work—and which they take home when they knock off. It exists in the "higher realm", above the audible ring of the trowels and knock of the hammers, that realm of theory in which every craftsman and foreman reaches out to a heavenly perfection, where no chisel slips and nobody sets out a job off centre, where all trades finish on time, and all quantities and costs exactly fill the bill. It is most emphatically not the network of plans and . sections, levels and falls, standards and finishes specified by the architect.

It is important to include in this "theoretical" systemisation on the site (that is, in the third sub-paragraph), not only the skill and the cunning of the tradesmen, but also the organising powers of the managers and foremen. In the field of production engineering there should also be an exact correspondence; not alone the skill of the machine tool operators and the fitters, but the leadership of the charge-hands, the organising skills of the store-keeper, of the progress chasers, and of the men who watch costs; above all, the ability of the shop and section managers who co-ordinate the work of the whole. It is in the codifying abilities of these managers, foremen and subordinate officials that the harmonies of productive operations have their most direct and important expression.

It is also regrettable that in these very directions British industry now faces one of its greatest needs. Those who know the present condition of the building trade are only too well aware of its fatal weaknesses; it is the gross ineptitude of its practitioners at Stages (2) and (3) above that will delay Britain's economic recovery more than will any other of her current ailments. The supply of drawings and other information by the architect, and the organisation of site operations by the builder, can be shown by operational research to create most of the industry's present troubles. In a way this is not surprising, as there has never been any systematic training or education emphasising these aspects of achievement; in particular, it has not been clearly enough recognised that Stage (3), the control of site operations, is neither Stage (1) or Stage (4). Those put in charge of it are normally good craftsmen or engineers thrown, uninstructed, into these systematising jobs, in which craftsmanship or a knowledge of technical design is no necessary qualification. We have as yet evolved no systematic study that might for convenience be called "Operational Methodology", an important part of which would be control of work flow through the points of production. This is due to the persistent belief that the "theory" side of productive operations is the architect's or designer's planning of the artefacts to which these productive operations give concrete form; in consequence, the gifted boy on the workshop floor has been encouraged to study so-called "theoretical" planning or design, rather than "theoretical" work organisation and control. Courses at technical colleges are almost entirely concerned with actual trades, which are in our fourth sub-paragraph, and the theory of planning, which fall in the first. At the present moment the architectural profession is feverishly trying to teach its members how to organise themselves and their relations with others in the building industry; this is in fact to stress Stage (2).

Within the universities it will be objected that the problems of practical achievement—of co-ordination between salesman, designer, production planner, purchaser, manufacturer, controller, accountant and so forth—lack the corpus of principle demanded of a university subject, that all this multifarious activity is only the extension of common sense, for which any type of education, including no education at all, may provide adequate understanding. There is a sense in which this is true. But to one who has tried to grasp the problems of making, say, a hundred articles each with a million separate components drawn from fifty thousand different storage bins, in a programme spread over two years (a not unusual task in industry today), it is also the sense in which Einstein's theory was but an extension of the multiplication tables, in which writing the works of Shakespeare was no more than an exercise in spelling, and the composition of an orchestral symphony is merely the next step after buying the blank manuscript.

Our consciousness reads the flow of time as activity. Whether we are waiting, half asleep in the early hours of the morning on Stalybridge Station, for a connection to take us to Huddersfield, or whether we are exerting the last ounce of our strength to fill off a stint of coal, we are *doing* something. And our awareness that we are doing it, or our plan or habit in accordance with which we do it, is part of the activity itself. Knowing what to do and how to do it is bound up with performance itself, and cannot be known intuitively. It is a great error to assume that theory and practice, knowing and doing, belong to different spheres of existence, or to different orders of awareness, but it is a common error, and leads us to ignore or undervalue the need for the physical planning of a job in concentrating on the visible execution of the job itself. In addition, it has deflected attention in industry from the improved co-ordination and more economical control of working operations, by concentrating upon the improvement and perfection of engineering form and technical design, without necessarily achieving high standards in the scheduling and programming of that design. In the result industry and society have many classical architects, but few site managers; many expert designers but few first-class production engineers or workshop foremen; many colliery surveyors, but a shortage of good under-managers; many historians of forgotten wars, and many interpreters of the human genius, but few men who can suggest what to do in the constant conflict between group and faction that bedevils our industrial life; in particular, Britain has fallen behind America in the effectiveness with which it can carry out the productive routines of industry. We may still produce our share of theoretical physicists, to read for us the generalisations of Nature as a whole; but we have not yet given ordered study to the limited and mechanic operations and methods of our productive specifications or factory routines. As Dewey has said, "The separation that has been instituted between theory and practice has had the effect of distracting attention and diverting energy from a task whose performance would yield definite results". It is these definite results of which our disorganised industrial economy stands in need today.

THE PATHOLOGY OF AUTOMATION

There is a tale by Hans Christian Andersen of a mechanical nightingale, whose exact and repetitious melody so enchants the artificial court of the Emperor that a law is passed to forbid the living bird from whistling its untidy song within the palace gardens. All are agreed that the wisdom of this law is matched only by the brilliance of the new songster, whose inventor is granted all those favours and rewards that the imperial court alone can offer. But one night, when the old Emperor lies ill, feverishly whispering that only a song will make him better, the mechanical nightingale, instead of reproducing its expected programme, splutters out the broken signals of catastrophe, to fall silent. The mechanics, the engineers, even the inventor of artificial nightingales: all alike are helpless. Nothing can be done. The Emperor turns his head to the wall and weeps. And so the court remains, in angry condemnation of the unhappy inventor, until the real nightingale returns to sing once more in the tree beneath the bedroom window.

The story, it is true, is not of automation but merely about a machine; the artificial bird had but one song and one input to start it. Even the juke box with (God forbid) a thousand disks is not a piece of automation, but merely a machine of multiple choice; the truly automated bird would need some biophysical link with its Emperor, directing it to sing or not, and, if to sing, then what kind of song, in accordance with the patriarchal mood. This should not be difficult, since it is now known that mood affects endocrinal activity and this in turn influences certain physical parameters, such as the electrical resistance between particular areas of the skin. But Andersen makes his point well enough; although it is a hundred years since he wrote his gentle ironies, there are few contradictions between Man and his Twentieth Century Technico-Economic Wonders not clearly foreseen by this melancholy realist. Civilisation, he shows us, is a marvellous contrivance, until it goes wrong. And since civilisation is, in the social field, what automation is in the technological, we may expect to see many parallels between the breakdowns of societies as organisms and the failures of such devices as the mechanical nightingale. We may try to build self-regulating societies; we may try to build self-governing mechanisms. But in each endeavour we must be on our guard against trouble; the more one relies upon the man-made law or the man-made machine the greater may be the disaster if the system fails. The British devised a machine of parliamentary democracy suited to Nineteenth Century Westminster; some are not surprised that it does not function in Twentieth Century Delhi. The Atlantic liner was perfectly adapted both to the leisured habits of the Edwardian first-class passenger and to the impoverished necessity of the Ukrainian emigrant; it has little place in an age of speed and equality. And when it sinks, as did the Titanic, just as when democracy has to be reinforced with machine guns, the cost may be calamitous. The bigger the basket the more eggs it may hold, but the more to get broken when the basket is dropped . . . not always by accident.

But pathology, or the study of things going wrong, is in itself a highly suggestive occupation. We may regard it as the investigation of the difference between what we plan to happen and what in fact does happen. When we say that a man is ill, or that a machine has failed, we do not, of course, mean that our expectation of illness or of failure should be zero. But we know, as a matter of simple observation, that other similar men are not yet ill, and that other similar machines have not yet failed. We are thus entitled to examine the difference between the ill and the not-ill, the failed and the not-failed. This examination we may call an exercise in pathology; in the study of our own selves we can assert with confidence that what we know of normal health and balanced function is largely derived from our investigations of disease and aberration. We should be particularly interested today in the pathology of organisation; as, with increasing technical knowledge, we attempt to build systems of increasing complexity, so we ought to give more and more attention to the relationships between their separate parts. A spot of rust on the mainspring of the mechanical nightingale or a nest of mice among the punched cards can start a lot of disappointment. But in the hour of technological triumph, with the medals still glittering on our breasts and the notes of the national anthems still ringing in our ears, we are inclined to look upon system-failure as an irritating but avoidable mistake, the consequence of carelessness, something that will not happen again. This is a cowardly as well as a shallow view, and grossly underrates the magnitude of our problem.

The Mythology of Systems Building

The need to submit complicated endeavours to rigorous test before putting them to everyday use appears in the first chapter of Genesis. Here we are told, in thirty one short verses, that God carried out seven major inspections of the system He was building: of light (v. 4), of the dividing of the waters (v. 10), of the vegetable kingdom (v. 12), of the solar system (v. 18), of birds and fishes (v. 21), of the animals (v. 25), and of the world as a whole (v. 31). There are not many examples of equal care being taken to ensure that satisfactory standards are built into the system from the very start. Nor is this all. The compilers of Genesis were fully seized of other problems that confront the modern engineering team; they describe the setbacks of their own Cape Kennedy, when they tell us in Chapter IX that, on the plain of Shinar, the generations of Noah set out to build a tower reaching up to heaven; God, observing these overbearing ambitions, argues that, should they succeed, "nothing would be restrained from them which they have imagined to do". He thus sets out "to confound their language, that they may not understand one another's speech". Thus "they left off to build the city. Therefore is the name of it called Babel because the Lord did there confound the language of all the earth. . . . ."

It would be hard to describe more truthfully the hindrances to communication that beset most sizeable projects today, whether they should call for cooperation between functional experts or press to their limits the resources of modern technology. Automation endures, no doubt, many humiliating vicissitudes, but in any catalogue thereof the failure of communication must occupy a consistently high place. The inability of men to agree, not only upon common ends, but upon the interpretation of common facts, is no less frequent in the laboratories of the Atomic Energy Authority today than it was upon the plain of Shinar five thousand years ago. And later, in the book of Samuel, we find another singularly modern chink in the armour of human achievement; the apparently indefatigable power of Goliath, in his coat of mail, with a spear as heavy as a weaver's beam, a system embodying all the latest advances of military technology, is brought to the dust by a boy with a stone. It is the parable of the battle cruiser sunk by the frogman with the plastic mine; of the red coated fusiliers of George the Third, drilled to the unimaginative and clockwork regularities of the barrack square, picked off by the sharpshooters of General Gates before Saratoga. The boy David, like the sniper and the frogman three thousand years later, defeats the greater physical power because he has a better understanding of the total situation. In terms of modern cybernetics, his receptor mechanisms are more selective than those of Goliath, so that he receives inputs more discriminating about his own outputs; he thus commands a greater capacity to learn and so to adapt, and in better adapting to the surrounding needs, can displace his rival. The parable of David and Goliath anticipates the triumph of automation over mechanisation, of the Second Industrial Revolution vanquishing the First, of Manchester as the cradle of the electronic computer with the stored, self-modifying programme replacing Manchester as the cradle of the factory machine powered by the factory steam engine. But there is no final triumph. The Manchester of the Atlas computer may be a better place than the Manchester of the satanic mill, but God had already decided upon the plain of Shinar that man's powers were to be limited, and even the contrivances of Manchester are to exhibit their limitations.

The Victories of Mind over Matter

The progress of automation, that triumph of mind over matter, expressed in the parable of David and Goliath, can be traced in the development of the steam engine. The pressure generated by heating water in a closed container was employed as a mediaeval amusement, by exploding water-filled iron bombs over slow fires; when this same pressure was employed in the earliest pumping engine, it had to be admitted to and released from the cylinder by a human monitor, a boy regulating each stroke of the monster with a separate tug on the valve control. At this point in time Man had created a new machine, though a crude one, like the boat whose simple sail is filled by the wind. There is a true element of automation in the linking of the valve with the piston; the machine now takes the first step—or is given the first push—towards self-regulation. But whereas the primitive engine must come to a halt once the boy ceases to jerk open the valves, in its articulated form it must, at least in theory, run as long as the fire continues to burn, or as long as there is water to be evaporated. But the organic system, of fire, boiler, pump and valves, has now become all matter; mind, personified by the monitor, has, at least for the time being, run away to play with its little friends. How then shall it be known whether the system has gone wrong? Or *how* it has gone wrong? No doubt it has become self-acting, so long as it still self-acts; its little slave might protest that he had even made it self-controlling, and he would be largely right. He can leave the system to its own devices, safe in the knowledge that it will not stop for want of anything that he could have supplied. Except for one thing: he could have warned others, even if he could do nothing himself, should the engine fail, or seem like failing. This is the function of mind not possessed, in general, by matter, nor even by specific controls. Since the engine cannot report its own unprogrammed failure (that is, of any unusual kind) somebody must watch over it and be alert to signal for help. But this assumes that signals for help are recognised. They may not be. The master of the Californian said at the enquiry he thought the Titanic was firing "company signals", whatever they may be, not calling for salvation. This is the plain of Shinar once more; if men seek to extend themselves beyond their capacity they will be destroyed because they do not understand what they are trying to say to one another. . . . . To some extent, James Watt provides the immediate, if not the long term, answer; with his centrifugal governor he constrains the engine to run at a uniform speed, by cutting off the supply of pressure should it turn too fast, by amplifying the supply should it slow down. We now have two automatic linkages, one internal to the mechanism, the valve, renewing the supply of steam in the very act of consuming it, and the other external to it, the governor, settling the rate at which the mechanism shall run, and with them both the technique of control is seen to be established. But the question still remains "Who then shall control the external control?" "Sed quis custodiet ipsos Custodes?" How, in other words, is this average speed of the engine to be determined? Sometimes the answer is easy; if the engine is pumping water from a mine it will be made to run fast whenever the level of the water is high, and it will be stopped whenever that level has been satisfactorily reduced. By a third mechanical linkage, articulating the depth of the water to the setting of the governor, the speed of the pump can be automatically controlled by the depth of the water itself. The triumph of automated technology is, up to a point, complete, for the system need not be touched by human hand, once its standards of performance have been built into it. Such developments as the electric pump that also cuts off its own power supply when not needed (while the fires under the steam engine continue wastefully to burn) introduce nothing fundamentally new. Once decided—and the system has no internal discretion of its own in these affairs—at what maximum speed the pump is to act and at what water levels it is to start or stop, the system may be left to work on its own until halted or destroyed by mechanical faults, excessive wear or hazard and demand unforeseen by those who have established it. It is in the anticipation and treatment of these sources of breakdown that the pathology of automation is interested; it is thus a kind of residue, something left over after technology has done its wonderful best.

The Widening Horizon

Such possibilities of breakdown are remote enough within the primitive orbits of the mining engineers. When they do occur, moreover, they are normally of a kind that have long been familiar and so can be dealt with by near-automatic rules. It is only when the wider context changes, when Civilisation goes wrong, that the simple system of the mine is disturbed, such as when Polish prisoners of war, forced to work in the German mines, pour the acid from their lamp batteries into the bearings of the mine machinery. This is the plain of Shinar under emphasis and no automatic system could be expected to handle it. But consider a context less primitive than the pit. If, for example, the system is intended automatically to remove, not water from the sump of a coalmine, but human beings from the depths of a city to their suburban homes, the occasions of pathology may be both more frequent and more serious. The safeguards that surround the pumping system and that extend its useful life are the products of long experience; at every level its custodians, whether human or mechanical, have learned to improve their grip upon the custodians below. But of the hazards that await the automatic train, racing hundreds of Londoners every minute back and forth along the new underground line from Victoria to Walthamstow, emptying them at night from the centre of the city upon the dormitories ten miles away, sucking them back next morning, there is so far little experience. It is clear that no train crew is needed, any more than a crew is now needed on an escalator, even if, in its early days, a man stood at each end to help the hesitating riders; the train can be started and stopped, whether in the station or elsewhere, by a system of automatic signals; the flow of the passengers to and from the platforms can be automatically controlled, as it already partly is on the Paris Metro. Nor need the signalling system demand men in local boxes any more; given electronic controls the handing-on of the train from one section to the next by watchmen physically within those sections is as antiquated and full of potential error as the semaphore systems of Napoleonic times or the foot runners of the Persian Empire. Once it is grasped that the physical control of moving the particular passenger demands no more than opening or closing a particular switch, the whole system can, in theory, be run as well from the dome of St. Paul's Cathedral as by scores of signalmen in stuffy cabins scattered wide beneath the streets of London. And, even if fares are not uniform, and Britain preserves its principle that the further one travels the more one pays, it is not hard to contrive that any ticket bought at such and such a price by the passenger, from a slot machine at his station of origin, could automatically prevent him from passing off at any station beyond those permitted by that particular fare. But the public reputation of London's transport system depends not so much upon the ingenuity of its feedback loops, relays, switches and so forth, as it does upon the image of its past. When a system has been established a hundred years, from early steam locomotives belching flames through sulphurous caverns to train robberies involving over three million pounds, it is as hard for the public as it is for the employees to change its ideas about how a railway should be run: the driver and his fireman, wiping their hands on cotton waste, their engine snorting and coughing like a living beast; the signalman, stripped to the waist, sweating over his great levers with their 200 lb pull; the porter bawling out the destination of the train at the top of his voice; the ticket collector, with a myopic and suspicious leer at everything put before him: all these were as much of the railway system as was the journey itself. "No Bishop, No King" observed James I of England, opening the campaign of persecution that turned the Mayflower towards America. "No Driver, No Train" seems, to the modern children of Britannia, no less a statement of the obvious.

The Quest for Reliability

But driverless trains, like clockwork nightingales, must have their failings. How for example, is the train to be stopped suddenly if somebody on the platform falls upon the line? Technically the problem is trivial; a beam of light (or, in stations with long or curved platforms, several beams of light) if obstructed by a solid object could at once stop the train, just as the doors of a department store can be made to open automatically at the approach of a customer. But what is to be done if the signalling system fails and the train carries on in danger of hitting another ahead of it? This is easily prevented by interlocking the signals and the motive power. If the signal is at danger the power in the next section is off, stopping the train at once. There are scores of devices that, by demanding positive attention to be kept open, automatically close on failure and bring their systems to neutral; the so-called Dead Man's Handle, that must be held down against independent spring-pressure, in the cabin of the electric locomotive, is one example; the brake-shoes on the colliery winding engine are another, for these must be held open by the operator and will stop the system should he faint or be inattentive to his duty. If, of course, some part of the automated system fails that is no less likely to fail should the system not be automated—as, for example, should a rail crack under the hammering of the trains, driverless or not—the consequences flowing from it are, perhaps, correspondingly more inconvenient, because of the trouble, within a large interlocking system, of isolating one section for repairs of any kind, without to some extent disturbing all the rest.

Apart from seeking to avoid the inconvenience arising out of the very comprehensiveness of the total system by improving the quality of the common parts out of which it is built—specifying rails of a quality higher in the system integrated round one central control than in the system carried on by the makeshift agreements between local officials—the architects of automation must pay special attention to the perfection and reliability of their intermediate components. If the automatic train is to accelerate at such and such a rate, or if its doors are to open and close according to such and such a specification, it is imperative that in practice they should generally do so. The technology of the particular devices on which their action depends is sufficiently well understood for the systems of quality control necessary to their manufacture and assembly to be both specified and installed. There are, of course, limits of accuracy that need not be exceeded; if high spirited football supporters are inclined to force open automatic doors, or even higher spirited ones to smash their windows, so that the coaches are out of service one per cent of their time on these accounts, it is throwing away money to aim at an internal failure rate of the door opening mechanism itself of once in, say, a million times. But how are these limits to be set for those parts of the system that, short of deliberate sabotage, are out of the reach of football supporters, even those from Liverpool? If the braking system of the train has, for example, to come into operation at such a place if the train should be moving with such and such a speed (and at some other place if the speed is different), how are the reliabilities of the various elements of the braking system to be specified? There is a starting point in the search. The automated system should be at least as reliable as the manually operated one it replaces, and since this, in the example of the automatic train, has behind it the wisdom of a century, we can agree that the standards are high. But there is no reason why, to enlist public confidence in the automated system, the failure rate should not be set at one tenth of the average experienced in the manually operated. Such rigorous limits are aimed at in the automatic landing systems of passenger-carrying aircraft. In the automatic signalling devices that will control the automatic trains the limits of error could very well be far lower: one hundredth of the frequency rate of the human signalman might not be impossible, even although on the most primitive single-track steam lines of Britain (where they still exist) the signalman's error is already utterly negligible compared with that of the local motorist. But a search for high reliability of component is the essence of pathology, since it must pose such questions as these: What goes wrong? How, if possible, does one stop it from going wrong? And if one cannot stop it from going wrong, yet nevertheless is forced to employ it, how does one still contrive to get along?

The Magnifying Power of Redundancy

The two parables of Genesis have something to say on this. There are, firstly, the standards of inspection of the piece parts: of the wheels, the axles, the brake shoes, the cables, the windings of the armatures and the alignment of the shafts; there are, secondly, the standards of communication of messages between these various parts, for it is in this that the success of automation largely consists. This is the myth of the Babel that failed, not because the bricks were of poor quality, but because the men whose task it was to assemble them did not understand each other, and thus their relative roles. A modern system of auto-mation may likewise fail if it is supplied with or generates within itself false, inexact or unintelligible information; one slip and the computer despatches its ten thousand accurately calculated bills all to the wrong customers, and it may take some ingenuity to build in safeguards against such mistakes.

One such is the well-known principle of the majority vote; at very critical points the possibility that an operator may be in error is allowed for by providing a number of operators at each of those points. If, of three men, among whom there can be no collusion, one reads an event differently from the other two, it may be necessary to decide which account is nearer the truth. If there is a record of a thousand triple and simultaneous observations upon which all three agree, such that the use of these observations shows the information they provide to correspond with external reality; and if these are followed by a triple and simultaneous observation, that two record as X and the third as Y, where X and Y are significantly different, which of X or Y is likely most accurately to describe the truth? It may not be possible, under the conditions existing, to take another triple set before acting, in order to find out whether the three observers agree once more, or whether one man returns a reading again significantly different from the other two, even if it would be reassuring to do so. But if we assume that the three men are reporting on the same event, we should be behaving reasonably to suggest that the two who observe X are "right" and that the third who observes Y is "wrong". Otherwise we have to assume that a rare event, namely, that any one observer should report a result different from his two colleagues, not having occurred once in a thousand trials, has now occurred twice in the same trial; and moreover that, should the quantity represented by X or Y be a continuous variable, the two simultaneous errors are of the same magnitude. It is possible that this is so, but not likely; it would be more reasonable to suggest that the observer reading Y is "wrong". Under this assumption we at once have a control device of very great power. If components, that receive, process and transmit information within our automatic systems, are individually liable to error they should be spread around with a lavish hand, and so ganged together as to record their majority vote; the system will then behave as if its components were more accurate than in fact they are. We note that the validity of this depends upon the independence of the separate observations; if the three men were responsive to common influences, apart from the events they are observing, such as bribery, coercion, prejudice, for or against certain elements in these events, or if they agreed, whatever their observations, to send in some average reading, such a control device would, of course, be useless. But as a means of improving the reliability of automated systems it obviously has a future. With such stratagems of deliberate redundancy at our disposal it is possible to think of automatic aircraft landing systems that are ten times as safe as those under the hand of the human pilot; it should be possible to operate at a level of risk as low as failure but once in ten million landings.

The Human Longstop

In the game of cricket a man of great importance, the wicket keeper, stands over the stumps as the catcher stands behind the plate at baseball. He should not allow the ball, delivered by the bowler, to pass him; if it reaches the boundary of the field of play, perhaps a hundred or more yards away, the batting side scores four runs. With an indifferent wicket keeper a fast bowler (who can be much faster than any pitcher, since he is allowed an unlimited run up and follow through) could thus be expensive, were it not permitted to place one of the other nine fieldsmen behind the wicket keeper. This is the long stop and his business is to stop the balls that the wicket keeper, by lack of skill or vision, allows to elude him; it is a place usually filled by the least distinguished player in the side. Men may take pride in their prowess as batsmen, bowlers, wicket-keepers, cover-points, forward short-legs, first slips, deep mid-offs, gulleys, third men; nobody, not even an Englishman taking a girl out to dinner in Detroit, ever boasted of his achievements at long stop. Yet the persistent problem facing automation is this: How are its long stops to be trained? For, just as Andersen suggests that civilisation is a wonderful contrivance, until it goes wrong, so also is automation. But when it does go wrong, and the wicket keeper allows the ball to pass, it is the humble long stop upon whom all eyes are focused. In the words of Psalm 118: "The stone which the builders refused is become the headstone of the corner". Yet the better the wicket keeper the less the long stop has to do and the less frequent his opportunity not only to shine, but also to learn the job. His position grows more ambiguous the less he is called upon, and, men being what they are, he may be so bored as to fall half asleep at the very moment he is most needed. This is precisely the fate of the human operators in the automated system; already the control of the generating station both by its internal instrumentation and by the instructions of the Regional Grid has so sapped the office of its superintendent of interest and initiative that the Generating Board is having difficulty in finding engineers of the calibre and vigilance to take charge of them—not only when the automated system is working well but also after it has failed and must yield back control to its local and separate parts. Each automatic train, too, must carry its own long stop, should the train be halted in the tunnel when the total system has failed. The passengers might panic if left without information, and there are obvious limits to what can be automatically communicated to the passengers of a driverless train beleagured in a crowded tunnel. And worse than panic is the unofficial action of the half-specialist member of the public; such men are common in Britain, and feel they have a responsibility to assume local control; they must be firmly dealt with by the long stop who personifies authority.

But if these occasions of emergency are rare how are the human long stops to be maintained? We may strive for automation to replace them, but the chance of unforeseeable error or unusual event must remain; the more complex and comprehensive the system the more an unexpected event in one part of it may do damage to the whole. We can remain alert with fire-drill and lifeboat-practice, but such exercises are often dismissed as mere pretence, the make-believe of children. In any case, they are the rehearsals for after the breakdown, not measures to prevent it; they are remedial, not precautionary, redemptive, not custodial. The question of who shall have custody of the custodians will always be with us. But the more effective the custodians, whether human or mechanical, the less there is to do for those who look after them. When the Royal Air Force had the custody of London's defence against Göring's bombers, the job of the longstops, or the civilian air raid services, became of indescribable boredom, night after night, week after week, month after month, of degrading inactivity; they remained boxed in half derelict shelters, always at the end of a telephone that had forgotten, it seemed, how to ring. The sirens that for others made the deserted streets of London echo with the voice of desolation, were to them fresh with promise, the awakening chords of some pastoral symphony, all springtime and youth. But how when nothing occurred for months, did one prevent these longstops from going mad with inaction? Since Britain was fighting for its life, we could force them to exchange posts, to change one deadness for another, as a prison governor might order a general post among cell occupants to ensure a change of scenery. Men with beards took up needlework and portrait painting; some made feathered angels for Christmas trees.

Since air raids are an emphatic example of Civilisation going wrong, there must be a parallel between this and the pathology of automation. There are some who suggest that education for leisure has become the problem; true, the devil still finds work for idle fingers. But in an automated age there are two forms of idleness: leisure and vigilance. We must not only fill leisure with interest away from work, but we must also maintain vigilance in our servitude at work, concentrating on the nothingness of normal running, springing into action at the instant of breakdown. The problem is not simply to escape the machine, but to monitor it; the computer firm has now its most difficult task in maintaining its products, simply because it may at any hour of the day or night need to call upon a highly professional longstop, alert, imaginative, resourceful. If the wicket keeper, in the form of the electronic controls, has let slip a million dollar payroll due in less than twenty-four hours, how does the longstop, or customer engineer, get to its help in time and what does he do when he arrives? Is the customer glad to see him? Or is he perceived as a herald to proclaim that his company does not know its business . . . . . and, moreover, that it never will? . . . This longstop is one of the characteristic figures of the age, like adolescent guitarists or professors of psychiatry. Like a concentrated residue from some atomic refinery he contains within himself all the elements of what the system does not need and does its best to avoid. But the greater the avoidance the more the residual concentration. The more we succeed in getting rid of the longstop the greater our need for him in emergency. The question again is how, as with air raid precautions staff, do we choose, maintain and improve the longstops of automation? . . . We may find it necessary on the automatic trains to provide them not with red lanterns nor shrill whistles, but with guitars and the more readable works of Freud. In simpler terms, we need to understand more than we do about the nature of attentiveness and the faults and emergencies to which it needs to be directed. For even if Automation is the triumph of Mind over Matter we must still enquire what Mind will have left to occupy itself when it has given Matter most of the responsibility for acting on its behalf. It cannot hand over the lot.

THE SCOPE OF MANAGEMENT CONTROL

The essence of the First Industrial Revolution was the application of mechanical power. Its tutelary genius was the steam engine. But this engine was not a *scientific* invention; its theory was not understood until long after the British railway system had been laid down; those who made early fortunes out of the locomotive had no idea *why* it worked. The essence of the Second Industrial Revolution is essentially scientific, and if we are interested, as managers, to understand what this particular revolution is all about, we must enquire into the nature of the scientific method. For the industries typical of to-day are based on scientific observation, experiment and control: chemicals, oil-refining, synthetic fibres, non-ferrous metals, aircraft, electricity, electronics, antibiotics, to mention some only. All these are informed with a spirit quite different from that of the industries of the First Industrial Revolution. In a sense, the difference may be thought of as one of accuracy. Whereas to-day any inventor would expect to machine the cylinders of his new engine to a thousandth of an inch or even closer, James Watt was content if the piston fitted well enough to let past a worn shilling, although he expected it to stop a new one. Yet accuracy is but a secondary effect, a consequence of science: the primary difference between then and now, a difference that is at once apparent to the student of the scientific method, is our grasp of the concept of control. It is the understanding and use of this concept that characterises science; it is in the area of control that modern industry has its greatest problems and its greatest opportunities.

It is now impossible for any scientist, so-called, to put forward a theory in the hope that it will be accepted without having to undergo the test of practical verification. The question is no longer, as once it was, "Is this theory interesting, or imaginative, or the product of a greater scholar or of a celebrated university?" It is merely, "Do the consequences of this theory turn out in practice to be what the theory declares that they will be?" The agreement of the results of the theory with those predicted by it, and not the reputation of its author nor of its author's patronage, is the criterion by which it will be judged. This requirement, that the suggestion or theory must survive the practical test, is the fundamental demand of the scientific method. It is also the basic concept of modern management, in which field it passes under the name of control. Just as the scientist must continually ask himself, "How do I test my theory, to know if it is true?", so the modern manager must continually ask himself, "How do I know whether what I am trying to do is of use in the world to-day; and how do I know whether I am really doing what I set out to do?"

In management, as in science, modesty is the necessary prelude to confidence; he who is to press his views on others must first learn to question them himself; it is a weakness of the traditional "case-method" of education for managers that it cannot permit feedback from any real situation, so that no argument can be tested in the experimental sense. It may teach managers to knock down the arguments of other managers, but it does not discipline them to attack the fortresses of objective fact. The mediaeval schoolmen needed to defeat only other schoolmen; the modern scientist must assault, even if with more powerful weapons, a world of external reality, contemptuously indifferent to his theories and mercilessly complex within itself.

These ideas are no doubt very general. It remains to express their relevance to modern industry, and in order to do so we must divide its vast field in some logical manner. Since the concept of control is, as it were, centred upon human wishes and has no meaning apart from its significance to human action, we must first examine the position of the manager himself, and show in what ways the concepts of control affects his relations to the systems with which he needs to work. These relations will demand that he knows of many things, that he has means of checking his knowledge of them, and that he is able to compare what he finds out about them with what he expected to find out. Moreover, in a good control system this information, or feedback, will come to him with a minimum of effort and a maximum of speed.

Systems of Control

We may list the main institutions with which the manager must work as follows:—

(a) *the manager's own self*. It may strike some as strange to regard the manager as an element in his own control system. For the present it will be enough to draw attention to the words of Jesus Christ in Luke IV 23. . . . "Physician, heal thyself . . .", where it is implied that the man who would improve the world must first assure himself of his own integrity. Some of the most interesting work in the field of control, certainly for those concerned with management education, is in this field of self-awareness and self-evaluation among managers.

(b) *other members of management*. There is evidence that many senior industrial managers in Britain to-day are much concerned with the stresses internal to the executive organisations within which they work. Factual information alone, even if flashed back by teleprinters

or meticulously logged upon daily reports, is not
sufficient for control in the full sense of the word;
markets, products, and techniques are continually
changing; cost, prices and quantities are continually
moving outside foreseen budgets; and decisions about
uncertain goals generally demand the agreement of
several different persons. In complex enterprises it may
be necessary for ten or more already overworked
managers to compromise, and where group relations are
poor this compromise may prove laborious, protracted
and uneasy. The improvement of such relations is
essentially a process of social learning, and successful
social learning depends upon the feedback received from
the investigation of difficult common problems; it is
thus dependent upon first improving the control system.

(c) *the enterprise as a whole.* The formal control systems
with which industry is familiar are generally designed
upon a scale comparable with the entire firm; the simplest
of all control instruments, the consolidated profit and
loss account and the balance sheet, embrace the whole
field of operations, although the various operating
budgets are necessarily departmentalised. There is
evidence to suggest that the effectiveness of organic control—or the extent to which the site or local manager is
able to integrate his activities with those of other units of
the firm, whether factory, coalmine, shipyard or steel-
works—determines not only how his technical operations
are carried through, but also the morale of his managerial
subordinates and of his labour force. Although controls
may primarily be introduced to economise in, say,
materials or the use of capital resources such as
machinery, or to maintain levels of quality or timetables
of manufacture determined by the design and planning
departments, it often follows that, if high standards of
operational control are achieved, they will be accompanied by an improvement in general morale; such

success depends, among other things, upon the size of the firms or units under control, since this usually determines the number of levels of management at which control decisions can be taken and the quality of the feedback that reaches them.

(*d*) *other competing firms.* A system of free enterprise claims to support competition between firms striving to capture the same markets. Traditionally, the control concept (where it has not been supplanted by price-fixing) has applied to the field of commercial competition mainly in the asking of some such question as "How is it that our competitors can afford to put this product on the market at a price lower than ours; or at a higher quality for the same price; or supported by an advertising campaign too costly for us, etc. . . .?" The whole fabric of economic theory that is built around "perfect competition", with concepts such as demand being a function of price, aims at understanding the market as a device that takes up various positions of equilibrium. This equilibrium is said to be determined by market forces; the price is said to be "forced up" or "forced down" or to fluctuate around an average. This suggests adjustment to impersonal commercial forces, which are said to exert "control". But this is not the concept of management control used in this essay. To exercise this we need to know the effects of our conscious and deliberate behaviour. For example, can the estimating department first learn in detail why its tender was rejected in favour of that of some other firm and then work on different lines next time? How far, if at all, does such-and-such a loss leader actually help to stimulate sales of other items? What *evidence* is there that the plastic toy costing less than a farthing captures a significant proportion of the breakfast food market? Does a statement that there is PL/13 in the toothpaste *really* have more sales appeal than that it contains Obsidium? And so forth. What are the feedback loops available to the marketing director? There have been several interesting developments in this field; one is market research, extending to such remote lengths as models of the national economy, and the response of a particular firm within a particular industry or its customers to the general level of economic activity; another is the so-called system of management ratios, by which firms in direct competition with each other for the same market actually exchange information to the advantage of them all;

(e) *the manpower market.* Every enterprise must be continually replenished with human beings, whether directors, managers, engineers, craftsmen, canteen workers, unskilled labourers, part-time cleaners, out-workers, or even public relations officers and trading stamp organisers; every management needs to establish sensitive understanding with the outer world from which it draws its men and women, whether engaging managing directors through expensive industrial consultants or snow-cleaners merely by chalking "Hands Wanted" on the factory gates. Indeed, there are firms faced with lopsided age distributions, among men as well as among managers, to whom control of these human inputs may well offer the severest challenge; the problems are not only those of engagement, but of training and deployment as well; they are not only those of pay, but of health and welfare; there is a strong impression, too, that the public image, or reputation, of the firm is important in determining its employment problems apart from the wages it is able to offer.

(f) *the materials-input market.* Every industrial activity, even among the primary producers like mining and quarrying, demands some form of initial equipment and the regular supply of working materials; in some industries, such as frozen foods or leather goods, the main element of success lies in the procurement policy. Knowledge of the market, assessment of quality, determination of sizes of lots to be bought, questions of transportation, storage, discounts, forward ordering and so forth all demand, in large concerns, rapid and sensitive systems of control. In manufacturing industry, the control of physical inputs often demands specialised knowledge of the subcontracting firms ready to accept work to be made out, and, where the parent firm has a reputation to maintain, complex questions of quality control may arise. Inputs to any enterprise, too, must include commodities more subtle than, say, cement or coke; they must include new ideas, new methods and even new kinds of raw materials, and all these demand adequate feedback to evaluate experience, to maintain schedules and to preserve estimates.

(g) *the products-output market.* It has always been essential for the business man to know the needs of his customers and their capacity or willingness to buy the goods he has to offer; the control of sales, and the techniques of consumer motivation research and economic forecasting are well understood. Any management that does not continuously receive accurate seedback about its customers' responses, whether of satisfaction or complaint, is unlikely long to prosper. Sometimes the product demands this by its very nature; for example, the manufacturers of a vaccine normally go to great lengths to gauge the impact of their product. Yet there are also those who are not, for one reason or another, adequately provided with the means of assessing their impact upon their clients; it is, for example, an obvious handicap for a textile salesman to be colour blind or for an export manager to speak no language other than his own. It is no less disastrous for an ironmonger not to know on which of his product lines he makes money and on which he loses it. It is idle to imagine that sheer volume of advertising will ensure adequate markets, since the evidence that advertising, itself a saleable product, generally stimulates sales, is far from convincing; advertising, in any case, is becoming costly. Moreover, in the last few years a new form of control has begun to appear in the product-output field, for the consumer's interests have become organised and, for a small fee, he can get accurate and discriminating information about the quality, price, performance and relative worth of many specific brands of commercial products. This is evidently a powerful form of information feedback, or of market control, and it will be interesting to watch how it develops.

(*h*) *industry and the nation-state.* Although the influence of British governments upon monopolistic industrial policies is not as strong as that of American, their intervention has at times been most effective; apart from this their powers extend to practically every field of action, and in some areas these are designed to assist and not to restrict; every firm of importance must regard its relations with government ministries and agencies, no less than with the nationalised industries, as an important sphere in which to exercise many forms of control.

This cannot be an exhaustive list of the networks of control that, like the web supporting the spider, *open out around a manager and his firm or department; there is, for example, no

---

*Some might prefer to imagine the control system as a family of Russian dolls, one within another; there is, for example, the economy within the nation, the market within the economy, the enterprise within the market, the production function within the enterprise, the manufacturing department within the production function, the machine shop within the manufacturing department, and so forth; to be realistic the dolls would often need to be twins or triplets, nesting together within their common mother. It is clear that the most difficult control problems will arise when several departments must collaborate at the same level; although all may be enclosed by another, each will tend to assert its own individuality and take unilateral action without informing its siblings; where the relation is one of complete enclosure the communication problem is simpler. It is well known that control *between* units is more difficult than control within the same unit; a skilful general, for example, will always attack his enemy at a point where commands are known to adjoin; a lawyer finds it easier to get witnesses to contradict each other than to contradict themselves.

reference here to the control of capital finance, although to be aware of its image in the eyes of potential subscribers, whether workers or shareholders, is a control objective of great importance, and certain notorious take over bids might not have been attempted had the feedback between directors and shareholders been richer. Moreover, in most businesses, particularly in retail trade, it is the money locked up in slow moving stocks that is often the most inexcusable source of capital embarrassment, and this is primarily a failure of control; there is only a scant reference to the relation between the management of a subsidiary firm and any holding company with which it is associated, although there are those to whom a consolidated balance sheet has all the delicate control—and hair-raising audacity—of a troupe of tightrope acrobats. Nevertheless, the eight forms of control listed above continuously press upon nearly every manager of reasonable seniority, and from each he must draw the information that enables him to answer the question . . . And, when I have at last decided what to do about it, how shall I know if I am getting the results that I anticipated?

Human Aspects of Control

In spite of what has so far been said, the first control need of the manager is not feedback about his costs, his delivery dates, his order book and so forth; it is feedback about himself as a person. How reliable is the image that he has of his own role and of his own abilities? Is he aware of the distortions that yesterday's experience (and, perhaps, tomorrow's expectation) may insinuate into to-day's perception, or of the inevitable bias that his personal values bring to his official decisions; or of the fadeless hope that the tricks with which he worked the greatest —and so most memorable—successes of his past are bound to come off once more? Or, more objectively, what knowledge has he of how he spends his time; or of the matters he attends to, as opposed to those he thinks that he attends to? Most highly-placed managers would find it hard to answer these questions, especially the first. When a man reaches the summits of top management his subordinate staff become cautious about letting him know of his peculiar habits; so long as he has managerial equals he may continue to receive useful, if sobering or unwelcome, feedback about himself, but at the very top he tends to walk alone. It is because they have learned to listen sympathetically to their husbands, for whom they are generally the only possible confidantes, that the wives of successful managing directors are such good neighbours at official dinners; a discriminating observer will often see the same influences in their secretaries. The industrial consultant, of course, is often the confidant of the managing director on more strictly business matters; there are many problems that the man at the summit would like to talk over with his colleagues, but that are so charged with personal and often embarrassing elements as to forbid him from doing so before he himself is quite clear about them. To think out loud may be dangerous when those of whom one is thinking may also be listening; there is always a place in the control system for a professional *alter ego* from off-stage. The chartered accountant often assumes this role, when, after the annual audit, he may offer advice about the conduct of the firm. But, in general, something more accessible and more wide ranging is needed than a yearly talk about financial policy; the problems of the top manager cover a spectrum of anxiety in which even if finance burns a bright and fiery red, there are other colours as well. However this may be, their isolation at the summit often leads executives to misjudge the use they make of suggestions from the shop floor; or to flatter themselves about their insight into the operational problems of their subordinates; or not to seek advice from their juniors as often as they think they do; or to dislike the man of less experience who has the courage to criticise his senior's views; or, in the big concerns, to undervalue the emotional dependence upon them of their senior staff. Attempts to identify these personal frailties within the managerial feedback system, and to make them known in a form—as on a tape-recording or through a statistically valid attitude survey—that is of real help to the senior manager, by giving him the picture of himself that others see in him, are among the more substantial promises of management research and education. It is admitted that the Gospel of St. Matthew expresses the same point;

> "And why beholdest thou the mote that is in thy brother's eye, but considerest not the beam that is in thine own eye? Or how wilt thou say to thy brother, "Let me pull out the mote out of thine eye", and behold, a beam is in thine own eye? Thou hypocrite, first cast out the beam out of thine own eye; and then shalt thou see clearly to cast out the mote out of thy brother's eye."

It is also important that the manager (for example, by listening carefully to a recording of his own conversations) should learn with what clarity he is expressing and forming his thoughts. If he is impatient when listening to others he will not easily learn to order his own thinking, since only by getting feedback about his own outputs can he be said to learn, that is, to rearrange the existing contents of his own mind.* The Epistle of St. Paul to the Corinthians says all that is necessary:

> For if the trumpet give an uncertain sound, who shall prepare himself to the battle?.... So likewise ye, except ye utter by the tongue words easy to be understood, how shall it be known what is spoken? For ye shall speak into the air.... Therefore if I know not the meaning of the voice, I shall be unto him that speaketh a barbarian, and he that speaketh shall be a barbarian unto me.

Every senior manager depends for his success upon the efforts of a team or organisation of subordinates; or he is, in turn, a member of such a team responsible to a superior. The three

---

*Current researches at Manchester suggest that the capacity of management to listen to their subordinates determines more than any other factor the general tone of the enterprise.

constraints of such organisations that may inhibit rapid and sensitive feedback are:—

(a) authority, or the nominal power of managers at any level to require that those of subordinate level shall carry out their instructions;

(b) functional specialism, or the requirements, whether formal or implicit, that a particular set of managers shall deal with certain aspects of a problem, while a different set of managers shall deal with others; and

(c) change, emergency, or innovation, which tend continually to disturb any arrangements that might have been formalised under (a) and (b) above; over-conscientious or inadequately informed attempts to catalogue the powers of authority and the respective spheres of functional specialism may, in changing conditions, soon lead to conflict and seriously impair feedback.

An organisation in which the management does not publish its policies but chooses to direct its operations by the continuous issue of short term and detailed orders to its staff is known as "mechanistic"; in times of economic, technical and social stability such an organisation can be highly effective, as were the Court of Louis XIV and many Victorian textile concerns. On the other hand, an organisation in which policy and its execution generate frequent consultation among different levels of management, and where persons of subordinate rank are expected to act upon their own initiative during emergencies, and are fairly supported even if their initiative is unsuccessful, is known as "organic"; it is the only possible type of stable enterprise in conditions of shifting emergency or unforeseeable change. Most industrial firms are working in these conditions today. Yet no enterprise can prosper under a senior management unable to allow its policy decisions to be influenced by discussion with or challenge from its subordinates, or fearful of encouraging initiative among them lest they make mistakes. The fundamental difference between survival and failure in conditions of change is a difference in the quality of feedback; it is through feedback alone that the deeper effects of change can be interpreted and mastered.*

In the final analysis the continuity of the firm depends upon its total adjustment to the economy in which it is placed. Although, in practice, most managers are concerned with local and particular activities—selling, manufacturing, purchasing, training and so forth—there must at all times be a concern for the overall balances between these separate activities. During the past decade there has arisen, firstly in America, but now also in Europe, the office of the controller, a senior manager whose business it is to organise a master set of budgets and accounts into which those of the constituent parts of the enterprises are to fit. It is his responsibility, before the year's work begins, to advise the directors whether or not the budgets can be integrated to form a harmonious working plan, and, as the year progresses, to draw the directors' attention to any areas in which this plan is not being fulfilled. It is naturally important to interpret this information about discrepancies between budget figures and actual figures with discretion and with sympathy. The budget must be used with care, if used at all, as an instrument of coercion for pressurising the foreman or the sales representative; secondary feedback must be available to suggest whether it is not perhaps the budget that, in the current conditions, is no longer realistic, rather than that the subordinate has fallen behind standard. It may be the goals rather than the performance that need amendment and the senior manager should be informed as to which; unrealistic standards invariably suggest lack of self-awareness, just as a man who complains about the shortcomings of his girl friends may do well to look into a mirror. A world-famous British firm, that has both developed

*One depressing result of research in this field is that some highly authoritarian managements get so little information about the effects they create that they might almost imagine their command an earthly paradise; their door is open to all who would complain, but none has the courage to pass through it. This is the same paradox of Nature as that the woman most likely to benefit from an improper suggestion is the one least likely to evoke it.

the electronic computer and installed it as an instrument of control over its own operations, has experimented here with the principle of Management Self-Accounting; field sales now exert a continuous influence, shared with headquarters, upon their own short-term budgets. Anticipated changes in local demand, known first in the sales areas, can be made known at headquarters in good time to influence both manufacturing and distribution schedules. There is still, within such a system of dynamic budgeting, plenty of scope for the headquarters to persuade the individual area, since headquarters will have the reported facts from the whole field; the individual area, however, now commands a channel through which it can, and is expected to, keep its ultimate targets reasonably consonant with its immediate expectations.

A Simple Model of the Firm

It would be laborious to list in detail the techniques used to-day by controllers and the persons who help them in their comprehensive task. But it is useful to regard any firm as an input-process-output system. All systems must both draw their resources from and return their outputs to the environment in which they work; an industrial firm draws from the world a range of inputs to itself, such as customers' needs, customers' money, raw materials, technical knowledge, human skill and so forth; it processes these in a wide variety of ways, and returns to the outside world the finished products, the wages of those who work for it, payment to the suppliers of its raw materials, and dividends to its shareholders. It also has many primarily non-economic interactions with its environment,* such as the tone of its television advertising, or any harm, such as littler,

---

*All interactions must, of course, have *some* ultimate economic equivalent; one can, at a price, forbid the sale of harmful products, if one knows first what is harmful. "Fanny Hill", for example, has been proscribed and its publisher has lost a great deal of money, or is said to have done so. But there has been no attempt to define precisely the harm it would have caused its readers, much less to express it in pecuniary terms.

noise or actual physical damage, that its products may cause to others; it may create a demand, by advertisement or selling schemes, that has little to do with any physical utility of its products, like the firm in Southern England that is said to sell tins of Highland air to expatriate Caledonians. It may be, on the contrary, a pioneer of some product that confers upon the public a sum of benefit far in excess of its own dividends, like the inventor of flea-powder, who died before his public had acquired the habit of using it. In addition to these three dynamic aspects of the firm's activity, there is a fourth, namely, to ensure that the resources now being used in the particular input-process-output system that is the present firm could not be used better. There are hence four main aspects of control of the total enterprise, namely—

(*a*) control of inputs;
(*b*) control of internal processes;
(*c*) control of outputs; and
(*d*) control of capital assets.

We may readily liken them to the activities of the individual; it must occur, sooner or later, to all intelligent men to ask themselves these four questions: "What do I want out of life? How do I actually live it? What results do I achieve? Ought I not, perhaps, to live a different life altogether?"

The input of raw materials and of human effort are dealt with specifically in later paragraphs; at this point our concern is with the market for what the firm has to offer. Are its products or services in demand, and, if so, how well are they provided? The basic parameters to be recorded are—

(*a*) volume of orders received;
(*b*) list of orders outstanding; and
(*c*) total of invoices issued.

These are fundamental. If the firm is not receiving enough orders, or if it is not collecting its money rapidly enough from its creditors, then it is unlikely to flourish, perhaps even to survive. For this reason, even the simplest forms of input control charts should not be despised, and every manager in charge of an output point, whether a sales director who rarely sees his customers or even his local salesmen, or a shopkeeper selling face to face over the counter, would do well to design, and keep up to date, a set of charts depicting the moving averages of the three parameters relevant to his main products or areas. The setting-up of such control charts throughout any enterprise would of itself be an interesting exercise in understanding the overall structure of its operations, and could well form an assignment for a middle manager in training for promotion to the ranks of the policy maker. Such control is desirable at any service point, not only at a sales outlet; "What has been asked for? What has been supplied? How long did it take?" Such questions are the foundation of all flow control.

It is in manufacturing production that the application of control can so far show its greatest successes. This is largely because production is, in a real sense, the simplest industrial activity; no matter how difficult the technology on which the process depends, it is lucidly easy compared with, say, accurately estimating customer demand, determining the optimum purchase quantity of raw materials and its most favourable price, or establishing intelligible communications with the workpeople on whom all management must ultimately depend. However this may be, this essay is not concerned with engineering or technical control, such as, for example, the optimal design of the products or the introduction of servo-mechanisms to regulate either the speed of machines or the pressures and temperatures of chemical reactions. Among the management controls of interest are those governing—

(i) the standards or accuracy of physical performance (quality control);

(ii) the extent to which plant and similar resources available to those in charge of current production are most economically employed to carry out the work actually demanded (allocation or assignment);

(iii) the volume of raw materials, engineering spares and

semi-finished stocks held in the enterprise to deal with current manufacture and with unforeseen demands or breakdowns (material or inventory control);

(iv) the amount of work, time, money or material consumed in making whatever has been specified in the design of the product (industrial engineering or work study);

(v) the wages and other costs accumulated in making particular products (standard cost accounting or, more recently, direct costing);

(vi) the flow of work through the enterprise, in order that the delivery of particular items is effected reasonably close to the dates on which delivery has been promised to the customer (production or progress control);

(vii) the renewal of the physical assets employed in these productive processes, to ensure, for example, that such assets are neither replaced before they have paid for themselves, nor are kept so long that their obsolescence and inefficiency are costing more than new assets needed to replace them (replacement analysis); and

(viii) the human performance, not only in terms of productive output, but also of attendance, wastage, sickness, accidents, pay claims, disputes, creative suggestions and so forth, of the labour force (personnel management).

We are also concerned with the overall success or viability of the enterprise, and must ask what has resulted from the original inputs, in the form of customer or market needs and credits, as they were handled by the productive and distributive processes. In a sense, this is the cutting edge of the control process. Have the results, both financial and strategic, matched expectations? To answer this question, a number of control instruments are commonly employed, the principal of which is the profit and loss account or the interim cost statement. It is, of course, to provide information for preparing these accounts that the skills of the bookkeeper are deployed; he is of late years powerfully aided by the work study engineer and the cost accountant, whose business is to measure in detail what has actually been done and what costs have accrued in doing it.* In many firms, the first need is not so much to establish accurate systems of recording, say the labour content (and hence the wages cost) of a particular item, as it is to examine the process by which that item is made, in the hope of reducing that labour content. In the same way, an accurate knowledge of the opening and closing balances of work in progress is not as necessary as knowing the optimum levels of such work at which the manufacturing superintendent should aim. Nevertheless, there is an informed opinion that the adoption of new ideas in British Industry is often delayed because the costing systems in use—and hence the effect of costs upon efficiency—are too insensitive to bring out clearly and unequivocally where the present processes are more expensive than they need be, and so suggest which should be replaced by methods promising to be cheaper. There is scope here for the control of those final charges to the producer, namely, distribution costs, and the marriage of work study to linear programming has produced new thinking upon such fundamental questions as the true cost of making a sale in a given market, and hence its effect upon pricing policy.

The Control of Capital Resources

The three previous sections have been concerned with the control of the enterprise to meet the targets that were actually set for it. How far did it complete its sales programme, keep to its estimated manufacturing schedules, and so forth? Even if all its predetermined goals were satisfactorily met, there remains the still greater question as to whether the goals that the firm set for

*Since the detailed construction of the profit and loss account (by improving the accuracy with which, for example, the costs of raw materials or direct labour are subdivided, measured and allocated) can be taken to great lengths, it is well to ask, in turn, what the cost of such accounting services may amount to, and whether they effect savings at least equal to their cost. The answer to this question is not always as simple as the accountant himself might be disposed to give. If line management employs a rough and ready system of accounting worked without professional book-keepers, it is uneconomic to suggest introducing, say, three cost clerks at a total outlay of over £2,000 a year if the estimated savings are not certain to exceed this figure.

itself were, in the circumstances, still the best available. It is not a question of whether or not the enterprise merely did better than last year. Even if it improved by three per cent, how can one be confident that ten per cent was not equally possible? It is not true that there is more joy in heaven over the one firm that improves than over the ninety nine good firms that, judged by existing standards, may need no improvement. In the industrial field, these questions are often answered by a second firm deciding that it could use the capital assets of the first firm to greater effect, whatever improvement may have been shown in their recent use, and there is a successful take-over bid. At other times a firm is driven to recognise that its traditional market can no longer survive, and that its capital assets should be employed for wholly different industrial or commercial purposes. But large and long-established firms, like large and long-established empires, do not readily respond to new influences, even if their significance has been suspected. An Austrian emperor, asked why he did not encourage the most evidently necessary reforms, replied "My administration is like the worm eaten timbers of an ancient barn; if I try to renew any part of it, the whole place will be round my ears". The industrial control problem arises long before the need to replace the entire barn or to sell its site for development by another entrepreneur; it arises not as soon as but before the first beetles are allowed into its timbers. It seems to be a law of nature, however, that the management unable to keep them out in the first instance is also unable to deal with them even when the edifice has reached the verge of ruin. The analogy is, of course, not complete; a firm, like the owner of a building, may decide upon total reconstruction long before bankruptcy or decay are threatening disaster. However this may be, it is a good control system that gives early warning of the administrative vermin.

There have grown up in recent years a number of consultant firms, generally staffed by econometricians and market analysts, who employ operational research to suggest better uses for the present capital resources of the going concern. Some of these methods are analogous to those already referred to under the control of production or output; on the other hand, since their estimates are concerned with the future and not with programmes to which the enterprise is already committed, their conclusions must be more tentative. The relevance of these forms of analysts (which may involve the construction of "models" of a national or an industrial economy) to concepts of control may not at first sight be clear. But the comparison of what one is doing, not only against what one sets out to do, but also against the best that one could do, is a perfectly legitimate exercise in control, and the sharpening of industrial competition following the abolition of retail prices maintenance will certainly demand an increasing awareness of the full potential of one's assets, both capital and human. An example should suffice; a very large farming concern in Britain, in spite of its present unquestionable profitability, has set out to examine the balance of its total activities. How should its wide acres be most economically used, not only in 1965, but over the next twenty years, given various possible developments, such as the entry of Britain into the Common Market, or a change in the policy of agricultural price support? This is an example of economic model building and, although the question may not be "Are we fulfilling our present policy?" but rather "Is our present policy the best one?", it remains an exercise in control, namely, in the comparison of what is with what should be.

Management Ratios

In August 1933 the American business magazine *Dun and Bradstreet Monthly Review* published an article entitled "Three Important Balance Sheet Ratios"; this article discussed the significance, for a large number of businesses, of the following ratios:—

(a) fixed assets to tangible net worth;

(b) current debt to tangible net worth; and

(c) funded debt to net working capital;

where the definitions of these parameters are as follows:—

   (e) fixed assets: the sum of the cost (or appraised value) of land and the depreciated value of buildings and plant;

   (f) tangible net worth; the sum of all outstanding pre-surplus and undivided profits less any intangible item in the assets, such as goodwill;

   (g) current debt; the total of all liabilities, due within one year from statement date;

   (h) funded debt; mortgages, bonds, debentures, serial notes and other obligations with a maturity of over one year from the statement date;

   (i) net working capital: the excess of current assets over current debt.

Tables of these ratios were published for large numbers of industries; these tables showed not only the national average for any given industry, such as paper making, but the upper and lower quartiles for all subscribing firms within that industry; a subscribing firm contributed anonymously to a common centre these three ratios of its activities. Hence any firm in the paper making industry having access to the data would be able to judge its own position within the industry as a whole. Under such a system of inter-firm comparisons it became possible for each individual firm to form this judgment without disclosing absolute information about its finances; it disclosed only certain ratios. Since 1933 the list of ratios published and used as control instruments has increased enormously; an example, Table I, shows those in common use in the American furniture industry. In 1961 a book by Spencer Tucker described a hierarchy of 420 management ratios that are said to be useful; a prudent manager would naturally limit the number he watched. There is a centre for interfirm comparison in Britain and some of the differences between the management ratios between firms of the same size and product line need to be seen to be accepted; there is plenty here to show in what particular timbers the worms are at work. There are, in the same retail trade in Britain, shops taking over £500 a day whose sales per square foot of floor space are as low as £5 a year, while others are over £100 a year; stock turnover varies from three fold to ten fold; and profit before tax as a percentage of capital employed from 1 to 20. And yet only a minority of firms subscribe to such schemes; the rest, it is to be supposed, are like those of us who refuse to visit the doctor because we may discover that we are ill, and, being wise people, know perfectly well that we cannot afford the luxury of sickness.

TABLE I

net sales to net working capital	6·63 4·31 3·06	net sales to tangible net worth	3·83 2·59 2·14
average period of collection in days	28 34 45	net sales to inventory	9·4 6·3 4·2
net profits on net sales	5·09 2·94 0·94	net profits on net working capital	21·0 13·8 5·03
net profit on tangible net worth	12·3 8·47 3·27	inventory to net working capital	53·2 69·4 105·0
current debt to tangible net worth	17·8 28·7 47·7	current debt to inventory	42·5 62·4 98·2
current assets to current debt	5·20 3·17 2·19	fixed assets to tangible net worth	21·2 35·0 49·7
funded debt to net working capital	8·4 19·3 40·9	total debt to tangible net worth	33·6 50·6 90·2

Table I, showing for the American furniture industry, 1955, fourteen management ratios:

Upper figure — upper quartile
middle figure — median
lower figure — lower quartile

Example

The firms constituting that 25 per cent of the industry

collecting its payments most effectively do so on average in 28 days or less; the median period is 34 days; the 25 per cent of firms least successful take 45 days or longer.

N.B. Some of these ratios are self-evidently expressed as percentages.

On February 16th, 1962, the British Broadcasting Corporation gave the first of a monthly series of television features entitled "Choice". This was a review, available to about five million people, of articles on public sale in Britain; the programme was based upon researches into their cost, quality and performance, conducted by bodies financed by consumers. The first programme was devoted to an analysis of the qualities of transistor radio sets and of fire-lighters, the second blankets; others have dealt with refrigerators and life-jackets; these were described by the name of the maker, the price, the performance and reliability and other features likely to be regarded by purchasers as important. Since 1957 such researches have been published in magazines one of which has achieved considerable circulation (*Which ?*—485,000 monthly), but here is a national form of sales control and of interfirm comparison in which the consumer holds the power. The particular feature of interest in Britain is that the programme is supported by a quasi-government institution, and any firm would seem ill-advised to ignore either the information provided or the need for control of their own products implied by such reports. It has long been a function of government to demand standards of safety in the workplaces of the employers; it is new to imply that the quality or value of the product is a matter of concern to the Government, no less. *Caveat Emptor* is no longer the defence of the huckster, but has become the clarion of the state.

The Control of Purchases

In some industries the factor most important to success is the purchasing policy of the individual firm. Where the cost of raw materials amounts to over half the total turnover the control of purchasing becomes critical. Where prices fluctuate on the open market or when demand for the final product promises to be high there is a tendency from time to time for firms to lay in excessive quantities of raw materials; in the result too much capital may be tied up in industrial stocks, and firms may find themselves unable to pay their bills. Table I shows that, in one industry, the interquartile range alone of ratios involving inventory is two-fold. A knowledge of the criteria by which to decide the regular purchase of stocks and to judge whether or not purchases should, from time to time, be accelerated or postponed is therefore of overriding importance in some industries. It is, moreover, often economical to arrange to the very hour the delivery of a particular part, nor merely to save storage or double handling, but also interest on the capital tied up in the part itself. The point may soon be reached at which a good scheduling clerk pays for his own keep, just as, in a previous age, the butler was worth his weight in gold if he could quickly pass off the redundant guest to a neighbour. The buying problem has many aspects, from the tactical procurement of materials for which there is both a variable demand by the firm's own production department and a variable market price, to the storage of engineering spares held against the random breakdown of key machines costly to have down beyond the repair time alone. Control becomes complicated, of course, when the delivery times offered by the suppliers vary from one occasion to the next; when different suppliers offer different discounts against different qualities or states of preparation of the raw materials, and when, as is inevitable in this imperfect world, a supplier with a good reputation fails to deliver or sends a consignment with more defects than the specification might allow. When we add the problems of renting warehouse space or the possibility of dividing large orders between several suppliers and remember that most firms purchase not one raw material but hundreds or even thousands, the importance of adequate control of purchases need be no more than hinted at. It is perhaps this very magnitude of the problem that discourages so many firms from facing up to it.

The supply of raw materials and the storage of semi-finished parts have become important fields for operational research. The rise of electronic computers makes it possible to handle today more readily than a generation ago the information relevant to these activities of management. Already the "theory" of an economic procurement policy is sufficiently developed; the problems are in the supply of data and in estimating the uncertainties of the future. The first of these problems should be solved in due course; the second, although it can never be solved in any exact sense, can at least be better understood by the methods of operational research. There are several basic concepts that need to be developed, and these include:

(a) the estimate average cost of being short for one day of one unit of the material under consideration;

(b) the cost of storing for one day one unit of the material, including interest, deterioration, rent, insurance and so forth;

(c) the estimate time-variability of demand for the material, expressed statistically;

(d) the cost of ordering and delivering the material in batches of different sizes;

(e) the estimated variability of price of the material, expressed statistically;

(f) the maximum availability of storage space;

(g) the reliability of the supplier both in quality and delivery, expressed statistically.

When the materials controller can collect or estimate this information he may be able to save up to 20 per cent of the cost of purchasing and stocking materials; this may be many times the cost of a system to control them.

The Control of Products

In a competitive economy any enterprise may need to examine

carefully whether the products that it offers to the market are those that, by skill, knowledge, capacity and reputation, it is best fitted to offer. This question has already been raised when discussing the control of capital assets, take-over bids and the place of consumer associations, but there is an aspect of it that calls for special attention. To what extent, even in a profitable concern, is the range of products made and offered for sale economically balanced? Even a casual study suggests that many firms tend to manufacture or market considerably too wide a range; such analysis has, since the war, thus attracted considerable attention under the title of Variety Reduction. The range in other firms may, on the contrary, be too narrow and a diversity of products could well be offered to customers without a corresponding increase in manufacturing cost. But the average firm, if it cares to analyse its total sales income by the contributions of its individual products, will probably discover that 80 per cent of its total income is attracted by 20 per cent of its products, leaving the other 20 per cent of sales volume to the more miscellaneous 80 per cent of products. It is not uncommon to find that 50 per cent of the products in the total range account altogether for less than five per cent of the overall sales volume; and keeping in the catalogue so many items (often several hundred) that contribute little, if anything, to sales turnover can be highly uneconomic. There is always a case for examining the final ten per cent of sales income in detail, and the records of every product that contributes to it should be so kept and searched as to answer the following questions:—

(a) is the demand for this item increasing?

(b) did the total sales of this item last year reach some arbitrary figure, say, £25?

(c) did the gross profit on these sales reach some other arbitrary figure, say, £10?

and, if the answer to all these questions is No, there is a *prima facie* case for removing the item from the catalogue; this is done, of course, not to throw away gross profits of less than £10, but because the same total effort put into a more popular item could lower selling costs and improve gross profits elsewhere. It will also pay a firm to examine carefully the 20 per cent of items in the product range that make up the 80 per cent of the total sales volume, since it should never be assumed that, because this minority of items accounts for the majority of the sales turn-over, each individually also earns a profit. While it is often said to be good business deliberately to market a particular product at a loss (the price of cameras has been held uneconomic to en-courage the profitable sale of film, and heaters the consumption of oil) it is as well to know which items are, in fact, losing money and how much; it often happens that such loss occurs uninten-tionally and, if the firm feels that it cannot raise its selling price, the least it can do is to discourage eager salesmen from pro-moting the losses unnecessarily. The periodical analysis of costs to this end is an example of managerial control of a peculiarly effective kind; the analysis is admittedly not easy and may lead management seriously to question the means whereby it allocates its overheads. It is most important that the accountant should be able to interpret such analysis from first principles.

Conclusion

The concept of control is essentially modern in its definition and its universal application, although, like all other fundamentals, it is as old as history itself. In all his conscious actions every manager should be able to defend, even if he cannot justify, the pattern of his behaviour, not only by describing what he is try-ing to do and why he is trying to do it, but also by assuring himself that, in the mirror of achievement, he can see his original plan reflected. The intention of this essay was, for example to exhibit those features of decision taking to which it is possible to hold up that mirror; it is for its readers to judge how far, in the event, this intention has been fulfilled. Control cannot be generated from the mere conviction that it is worth ensuring, any more than sin can be avoided simply by believing that one

should try to avoid it. But it is always useful to distinguish between the good and the bad, and one must be able to recognise
the situations in which control needs to be established or improved, and not all of these involve concrete observables such
as the number of customers waiting for deliveries or the loss in
value of rusty castings piled outside the foundry. On the whole,
the control of management activities that have so tangible an
outcome as these is comparatively easy; it is the activities that
depend upon more subtle features, such as the personal security
of the general manager or the allocation of overhead costs, or
that have less predictable outcomes, such as attempts to secure
the co-operation of foremen and shop stewards or to raise
income by modifying price policy, that provide the real tests of
control system. All we can safely say is that control is an attitude
of mind, a way of learning about oneself, a way of evaluating
what one is doing, but since, in this life, the most obvious
truths are always the most readily overlooked, there is no harm
in asking what this attitude of mind should be, and through
what self-discipline it is to be engendered. It is not true that
ostriches, faced with situation they do not like, will bury their
heads in the sand, but there may be something in the suggestion
that those who rule over large empires should know whether,
and, if so, how fast, the worms are eating into the timbers of
their financial roofs.

INDUSTRIAL RELATIONS AND INDUSTRIAL TRAINING

Historical Observations

Technical education, in the forms in which we now know it, has shallow roots in the soil of British industry. This was not always so. In the fourteenth and fifteenth centuries it was the personal concern of the employer, or master craftsman, to initiate his apprentices into the guild, and to give close attention to their moral and spiritual welfare during the long process. He was enjoined by his guild to treat the apprentices as members of his own family, and, for something like two centuries, the guilds themselves saw to it that the master kept his bond. But this system was already in decline before the famous Statute of Apprentices was passed in the last year of Elizabeth; it had ceased to mean anything at all by the first days of the Industrial Revolution and its death was legally recognized in 1835 by the Municipal Corporations Act. The great collision between capitalism and technology that, in the late eighteenth century, had made Britain the workshop of the world did nothing for technical education except to bury its corpse.

The ceremony of its resurrection must interest every one of us who today, in some way or another, earns a living by teaching (or trying to teach) industry how to do its many different jobs.

The late eighteen eighties had been years of comparative prosperity; this, in many industrial towns, was accompanied by an amount of drunkenness that shocked even members of the Government. The Chancellor of the Exchequer, Goschen, was determined to reduce the amount of alcoholic liquor consumed by heavily taxing both beer and whisky, to bring in a revenue of about half a million pounds during the first year. This income, which actually entered the Treasury, he planned to use for buying out some of the landlords of the public houses to be found on every street corner of our industrial cities. But, in the debate upon this application of the money, Goschen was defeated by an alliance of the brewers and the churches; the first objected to the closure of the public houses as a restriction of trade; the second could not agree that public money should be used to compensate men deprived of what, in their view, was a sinful living. Goschen was therefore left with money collected for a purpose denied him. He happened to be interested in technical education, and so persuaded the House of Commons to devote the money to that cause. Our present system of technical education thus comes as near to being illegitimate as anything can be; it is the child of this enforced union of the pocket of the brewer and the conscience of the church. It is from such episodes that we perceive the true attitude of our ruling class towards educating their mechanics. It is also instructive to compare the political implications of drunkenness in 1890 with those of lung cancer a lifetime later; technical education, baptized in the whisky money, might well be confirmed in the incense of nicotine.

The Division of Labour

We might ask ourselves why technical education was for so long (and still largely is) neglected by the very nation whose industrial output, in the early nineteenth century, exceeded that of all the other countries of the world added together. One reason might be the very success itself; a man who has to fight only small children does not pay for boxing lessons. But this is not all.

The present efforts of the British Government to force upon industry a duty to train its work people show how feeble is the conviction of the average employer that life in the workshop might demand more than the untutored faculties of nature. He has, he feels, removed the need for serious instruction by simplifying the artisan's task, following the demonstration by Adam Smith that, if one hundred men share out the total task of making one pin, it is possible to multiply their individual productivity one-hundredfold. This division of labour colours our national outlook no less than our industrial; it lies at the heart of many of the communication problems by which our society is bedevilled. It is clearly the stock-in-trade of the efficiency expert with his stop-watch; but it also buttresses the Bridlington rules, intensifies the venom of Orwell's 1984, fortifies the sixth form master in his plan to specialise, and makes mutually unintelligible the research workers of the Atomic Energy Authority. The division of labour seeks a triviality of performance that demands no skill, no judgment, no effort of learning; the operator is to become as much part of the process as the plant or the raw materials.

We try to ensure this, in the language of the work study man (himself but an inflated fragment) by "breaking the job down," and, in doing so, are not disposed to ask the price we pay for it in the invisible currency of social disintegration. But its long term effects upon the hardening of industrial morale do not need to be searched for; on inspection the albatross round the necks of our salesmen abroad may well turn out to be a tattered copy of The Wealth of Nations.

The Philosophy of Mechanism

These ideas of Adam Smith are valid, however, only so long as one is content to discuss such affairs as the manufacture of pins, or even of motor cars, in the abstract world of mechanical design. So long as it is possible to see the total task as the summation of large numbers of smaller tasks, each of which can be done by one person, one is entitled to think of the sum of the parts being equal to the whole. This follows, as it were, a proposition in elementary arithmetic. But it does not follow that in the real world, as distinct from the world of formal logic, the integration of thousands of different sub-tasks into a complicated final product is simply the microscopic definition of these sub-tasks in reverse. An engineer may see this finished product in his mind's eye; he can make a specification of it on his drawing board, and he can decide that such and such components must go into the final assembly. In a motor car there may be many thousands. He can specify of each part that it is to be made of such and such a material, of this or that particular shape; and that it is to be fashioned in such and such a way, on such and such a machine by a man who works first on this, then on that, now doing so and so and later working on such and such. The final specification of what is desired may cover hundreds of pages and scores of blue prints and parts lists. In their very magnitude such catalogues are always impressive. But their translation into an organic reality is another question altogether.

The engineer or the designer must so closely and exhaustively specify his objectives for a simple reason. The function of the machine or other artefact to be created does not exist in nature and is in no way a property of the inanimate materials with which its designer is working. For example, an engineer may wish to make a lawn mower for cutting the grass on his tennis court; in no sense does the steel of which its blades are to be made possess a desire to cut the grass, whereas if the engineer used a sheep or a cow on the lawn instead of a mower he would not need to simulate in it any desire to crop the grass; this would already exist in the animal. But the capacity of the mower to cut is a highly specialised quality indeed, and depends upon the most minute adjustment of the parts to the will of the designer. If a bearing is too stiff to turn or if the blades are too far apart the machine does not display any organic ability to adjust itself; the various parts do not possess any mutual recognition of their malfunctions nor any power to co-operate in curing them. The stiff bearing can continue only to jam, and the blades ineffectually to fly past each other, unaware that they should be in light contact, shearing sweetly through the grass instead of tearing some up by the roots and leaving the rest bruised and mangled. Hence, the human designer has to state completely and unequivocally both what is to be the exact nature of every single part (within certain acceptable limits of error) and what place it shall occupy in the finished product.

There is, of course, nothing new in this. The artificers of Biblical times had, in their way, to work as much in accordance with preconceived and detailed plans as does any mechanic in a refrigerator factory today. But we note that the first complex task on record, the Tower of Babel, failed, not because the piece parts were defective, but because the human problems of communication proved insoluble. It may be the subdivision of the final product into many discrete parts that enables us to use best the techniques available, but the problems of their integration remain. It is true that in recent years we have started to build highly complex machines that are, to a limited extent, self-adjusting; they exhibit the first hesitating steps towards self-organisation. They respond to changes in their environment in such a way that, without specific instructions, they continue undisturbed towards their goal. An ancient example is the self-righting ship; when a wave or a gust of wind tends to make her heel over the disposition of the ship's weight makes her swing back again. A more sophisticated example is the windmill that turns itself into the wind by the action of a tail wheel alone; or that adjusts the speed of rotation of its sails to the varying force of the wind by altering their angle of feather. These are all primitive illustrations of the automatic control mechanisms that have developed today into systems of continental defence using electronic computers ganged together while standing thousands of miles apart. The fact remains that these are still mechanisms constructed to the precise specification of their designers; the recovery function, like any other, must be incorporated from the start, and, in the context of this essay, its

10

incorporation greatly complicates the assembly of the mechanism in the first place.

Mechanism and Technical Education

The philosophy of mechanism, simply by its astonishing success, has had, it would seem, all the vindication that might be demanded. The rocket *has* passed the moon; it is no longer a romance of Jules Verne. But it can claim to have succeeded not only because the designer could so break the total task down as to satisfy each of its component needs by an appropriate technical artifice, but also because, as Adam Smith pointed out, each technical artifice could be allocated to a particular individual so skilled in its execution that his potential productivity became limited in the end only by his physical endurance. And even this in turn could become the subject of microscopic specification. Not only was a labourer to spend his life shifting iron castings from one point to another because the transfer of these castings was one step among one hundred thousand others in the production of a steam engine, but his exact movements became the subject of analysis so that he could move his castings without using his time in non-productive effort. He could be taught, in other words, the most economical movements of his arms and legs in order to accomplish his task in the shortest possible time. The mechanistic outlook of the designer penetrated beyond the artefact itself; it entered into the control of the human slaves who made it for him.

This, essentially, is the Platonic idea of technical education. It is to instruct its students how to perform certain mechanical operations as the necessary components of some greater or collective achievement. The firm that is to make tractors, for example, must have artificers of many kinds and, according to the extent to which the philosophy of mechanism exercises an ascendency over the firm, so are the individual skills of its workpeople to be fitted into a fragmented programme based upon the technical design of the tractor. There is a demand for this man to make certain marks on a sheet of transparent linen; for another man to assemble certain pieces of wood to form a pattern of sand into which certain other men will pour certain molten metals; others will be needed to put particular pieces of metal into such and such machines; and so forth. At this level of subdivision the task of the director of the technical school is simple, since he knows precisely what he is trying to do. He is trying to teach one man how to shape this piece of metal with a file, another man how to shape it in a machine and still a third man how to shape it by some treatment that also changes its nature under the application of heat. At some other place in the building other men will be engaged not in the practical arts of shaping metal but in listening to lectures upon what is called the theory of metalworking, that is, they will be hearing what different methods of shaping metal have in common, and where they differ. In still another place a third group of men will be studying the effect of putting this or that metal into one or the other liquid; the exact metals and liquids they bring into contact will determine whether they are studying chemistry or electricity. But we observe that they are merely trying to learn how better to occupy some position in the long chain of events that go into the making of the industrial product. Even if the men are quite senior persons, who already know the effects of dipping particular metals into particular liquids, or about the results of pouring particular metals into particular moulds, they may still take further instruction in the arts of assembling those various sub-artefacts. These, in general, are concerned with the time it takes to move pieces of metal, or wood, or plastic, or even asbestos wool, from one place to another and to fit them together in particular ways laid down in the overall specification of the final task. But these superior men, who are often distinguished from the others by being called managers, are not in general taught anything essentially different from the craftsman or other subordinates more directly concerned with the physical operations of the metal-working proper. If the potential craftsmen under a system of technical education may be thought of as learning their alphabets, the future managers are simply learning how to spell. The man who has taken a doctor's degree at a university by original research in some branch of technology—which may be taken as the summit of our system of technical education—has merely shown us that he can construct at least one sentence in the technical language. But he may still discover, when he takes a job on the factory floor, that this is quite inadequate to describe what is going on, especially to describe the actions of those who work on it.

Technical Education and Industrial Behaviour

After long years of technical achievement in industry the interest of the public is now turned upon the factories where that achievement is to be found. There are, in the main, two reasons for this. Firstly, the occasional property-owning democrat may wish to learn from first-hand observation exactly how, say, his new motor car has been made. His first impressions of the manufacturing process, minutely subdivided until particular men may be seen throughout a whole day to do no more than operate presses that make small holes in pieces of metal of unidentifiable shape, are probably of surprise, that men should be found who can endure to do such work, indeed, who are said to refuse any other. In more than one man this surprise gives way, before the end of his visit, to a thankfulness that he himself earns his living differently; he may be encouraged not to take too pessimistic a view of what he sees by the personnel manager's assurance that the men he is looking at are oblivious of their real task, and are thinking of what they will do away from the work situation. Nevertheless, the doubt stays in his mind. Is this, he asks himself, how we are spending our lives? Does his own task of checking insurance policies or giving lectures in cost accounting, appear as sterile to those who see him doing it, as the tasks of these car-workers seem to him? Is the broiler-house so different, after all?

The second reason for public interest to be focused upon those scenes of technological triumph is that, without warning,

like the eruption of Vesuvius over ancient Pompei, some calamitous avalanche of hatred may overwhelm the actors. Ten
thousand men suddenly refuse to work; the whole roundabout
is brought to rest as if a power switch had been pulled by some
giant hand. On enquiry one finds that one man has objected to
another making a mark with a piece of white chalk upon a particular piece of metal. Further enquiry reveals that every man on
the payroll could chalk to his heart's content upon the factory
wall, or that some other man could make the mark in dispute
upon the same piece of metal as boldly as he pleased, without
exciting any hostility whatever. This may at first strike some
external observer as odd; the public, who in general know little
of these affairs, are led by their newspapers to believe that the
men who raise these objections are peculiarly vicious people;
they are described in the press as avaricious and unpatriotic and
their vices are paraded in catalogues overlooking no item of
depravity. But it may be seen, by the observer who cares to look
a little deeper than the account of the journalist, that nearly all
the men who work in concerns based uncritically on the division
of labour and the philosophy of mechanism display, to some
extent or other, the same explosive potential. Yet since this has
nothing directly to do with dipping particular pieces of metal
into particular kinds of liquid, its study does not enter any
system of technical education and so remains largely unexa-
mined by those engaged on the microscopic sub-divisions of
design and process.

Nevertheless, the purveyors of technical education are not
entirely satisfied. One of the many surprising things about this
social service, as surprising, perhaps, as the alcoholic circumstances of its birth, has been, and still is, the unending correspondence in the press about the need for the liberal education of
technologists; those who have taken courses of technical instruction alone are, it is suggested, still deficient in certain qualities
essential to the successful control of the human process. If, it is
thought, just knowing about the effects of dipping such and such
metals into such and such liquids leaves the student still in the
dark as to the nature and origins of the avalanche, then there

may be virtue in teaching him something of the less mechanical victories of the human spirit. Hence we find leading figures in the world of technical education writing articles of questionable literacy upon the need for teaching gas fitters something about Elizabethan drama or Austrian string quartets. Technical colleges and colleges of advanced technology are suddenly advertising for Directors of Liberal Studies, and a new profession is created overnight. Not the least surprising feature of this educational pageantry is the cultural level of those engaged in it. If any proof were expected of their knowledge of, say, Shakespeare or Mozart, it would be in their belief that the works of these men necessarily exert some direct or even immediate therapeutic influence on the work situations of coalminers or of men who dip metals into liquids. It is the belief that, because some historical plays or chamber music are to be ranked among the finest products of the imagination, an acquaintance with them must necessarily slacken the desire for industrial conflict; it reflects the faith of the cannibal who sucks the blood from the heart of his enemy to acquire his strength.

The Constraints of the Technological Imperative

Whatever may be the human skills of industrial managers, the fact remains that, so long as we want such products as tractors, motor cars, refrigerators, television sets and so forth, and demand that they shall be cheaply available, it will be necessary to accept the decision of the technologist upon their methods of construction. The philosophy of mechanism must, moreover, demand some division of labour. At the present level of our industrial development it is unrealistic to suggest that we should abandon motor cars in favour of, say, sedan chairs, or that domestic entertainment should cease to rely upon the television set and seek its fulfilment in, say, charades or amateur conjuring performances. It is equally unrealistic to think of television sets being made in some kind of William Morris Arcadia, with craftsmen in homespun clothes singing at their anvils. The conditions of technical progress include those constraints of human activity demanded by the technical methods of which we are masters. If these specify that certain pieces of metal must be dipped in certain liquids before they acquire the properties that their function demands, then there is no avoiding this simple fact, however monotonous or unpleasant the dipping process may be.

The responsibility of the industrialist in whose factory the process takes place is of indescribable complexity. Seen purely as a piece of technology, as something taught in a course for, say a national certificate in chemistry, his task may be a simple one; it may be discharged quite adequately if the temperature and concentration of the liquid and the cleanliness of the metal have reached such and such standards. But after a particular man or woman has performed the task one hundred, or one thousand or even one hundred thousand times, he or she may, without notice, cease to want to do it; he may even walk out of his job for ever and without warning. Or the human operator may do the task badly, splashing the liquid where it is not wanted, or failing to immerse the metal to the exact extent specified by the technology, so that errors appear in the final product and lead to bad feeling on the part of the customer, or even actions at law. Or the worker may be dilatory and rarely have enough pieces of metal ready when they are needed; in consequence, important orders, worth more than any single piece of dipped metal by itself, are lost. And if the worker is discontented with his task or with the payment he gets for it, he may infect other workers who had previously been quite willing and cheerful, so that, when some misunderstanding arises between this particular workman and his manager, the tensions will be shared by others and the whole factory might come out on strike. The effects of this might include a loss of output equal in value to the original cost of drawing up the technological specification of the product. To ensure that the conditions of total achievement, rather than of technical necessity alone, are satisfied at the place of work, the manager has a task towards understanding which his knowledge of what happens when metals are dipped in liquids makes only a partial contribution, often, indeed, no more than a marginal one. This is the true field of interest to which the exponents of technical education must give their attention. It will increase the difficulty of doing this to pretend that the solution of this major problem has to do with what is now being offered as liberal education, so called. We have to rewrite The Wealth of Nations, not reissue it as a paper back.

The teacher is handicapped not only by our general ignorance of factory problems and processes, other than at the level of the journalist; there is reluctance on the part of industrialists to permit the pathology of mechanism, in this wider sense, to be examined objectively. The failure of purely technical processes can be studied in the laboratory, and an accurate knowledge secured about any changes of operating parameters needed to bring such processes back into control. But the failures of the total systems of which the purely technical operation is no more than a part must necessarily imply human failure, and this is by no means easy to examine dispassionately. One does not offend an electric circuit by tracing the weakness within it that led to breakdown; nor can one insult the law of gravity by suggesting how it caused to fall over something that, in the operating plan, was supposed to stand up. But human operators, whether or not in the ranks of management, are not so devoid of emotion as are volts or foot-pounds; they will normally resent strenuously any investigation of what is going on around them if there is the slightest chance that they may be found responsible for its failures.

The Human Needs of Technical Education

This brief description of the problems of industry that lie outside the field of technical instruction as we now know it, that is, of the specific study of physical, chemical and other techniques, might, at first sight, suggest so wide an extension of the curriculum of the young technologist as to lose sight of his need for such instruction in engineering operations and processes. It would, moreover, be impossible, even if there existed an ordered knowledge of the human forces of industry as distinct from the laws of, say, engineering, to teach it all to our students in universities and colleges of technology. Nevertheless, there are several educational needs that, granted our wish to observe the technological imperative, it should be possible to meet; and that should be met, if necessary, by removing parts of any existing syllabus.

The first is, without any doubt, to engender the habit of reading. This is not necessarily to advocate the classics, for it would be progress enough to incline our students to read the literature of their own technology. A report entitled "What They Read, and Why" by the D.S.I.R., has emphasised the depressing fact that, even in those most progressive industries, electronics and electrical engineering, only a minority of technologists read anything at all and few indeed read original papers in their own professional field. To vamp up an interest in classical literature when the technical population is so near to being illiterate in its own fields is a major dishonesty. How the teacher of engineering is to get his students to read even the engineering press is a problem for the teachers; some of them might start by acquiring the habit of reading the engineering press themselves. It is impossible to feel that the vast incuriosity discovered by the D.S.I.R. is altogether accidental; it must have been partly engendered in the students by a negative example among their preceptors.

The second need of persons who are to take responsibility in this complex field of interaction between the human subject and the mechanism he controls is for an understanding of psychology and allied subjects. To attempt the management of men under the stresses imposed by modern technology without clear ideas upon such concepts as the sense of security, the attitude of the individual to authority and the nature of his defence mechanisms when threatened, is to walk on a battleground not only unarmed but naked, even, at times, as if stripped of one's very skin. It is particularly important that the manager should understand these qualities within himself. There is a considerable research literature in this field of which the young engineer should have a working knowledge: in the need for every individual to be a member of a stable group, both depending upon it and contributing to it, sharing its beliefs and prejudices, observing its norms of behaviour, joining in its defence when any of its members are attacked and so forth, and in the need to integrate the work around the group rather than the group around the work; in the need for every individual to know what effect he is having upon those around him, and of feeling that he can turn to any of them in the solution of his own or their problems; in his need to feel that he exercises control over his destiny by being encouraged to extend his own abilities or qualifications, either by formal training or by knowing that he can discuss his technical problems with his superiors, and, in the discussion, be accepted, if not as an equal, at least as a person; in the need for supervisors themselves to understand their own personality traits, and to know that they will tend to pass on to their subordinates the type of treatment they receive from their own superiors, unless they consciously take steps to do otherwise. There may be a need for some knowledge of anthropology; there are propositions about group customs, superstitions, values and loyalties that should be known to every manager. In particular he should be aware of the nature of status and of the need of the ordinary and undistinguished person to believe that he possesses it in the eyes of his fellows.

The Need for Systems-Analysis

The two needs of technical education so far suggested have both direct bearing upon the supervisor's own behaviour as a person. It is no less important that he should see himself in another light, that is, as a link in the long chain of technological processes that go to make up the final product. This may be looked upon as a river flowing smoothly towards its source, joined from time to time by tributaries in the form of orders, engineering instructions, raw materials, semi-finished parts and so forth. In a civilised country, the flow of the river is, to some extent, controlled by the lock keepers; in the same way the technologist, when he acts as a manager, attempts to influence the flow of work, by taking a man off here and setting him on there, holding up this job and pushing on with that, and so forth. The conditions under which management is permitted by the trade union to make these adjustments need a great deal of examination, but in general the less the specialisation the greater the flexibility; we recognise a number of fields of enquiry and of decision-taking important in preserving a satisfactory morale. There are four major classes of decision that any manager in charge of a flow system needs thoroughly to understand, all profusely illustrated in the literature of both operational research and of industrial sociology.

The first are decisions about queues, or of items waiting for service at moments when demand is greater than capacity; queueing theory has wide application and is concerned as much with desk matters waiting for managers to make their minds up about as it is with broken-down machines awaiting their fitter. The second type of decision affects replacement; its study throws light upon the choice of moment to interrupt a flow system so as to create the least total disturbance, and it suggests how far, if it is necessary to stop a plant to replace one element, it is also desirable to replace another, even if this seems still in good condition. The third general type of decision influences allocation; given such and such resources, and such and such jobs to be done on them, what is the distribution of tasks among the resources that minimises the total effort expended? Although this kind of decision, known as linear programming analysis, is properly the field of the electronic computer, there are nevertheless a few basic principles that can profitably be used by managers who have no access to one. It is even possible to solve some of such problems with a pencil and paper. The fourth type of system decisions are about spares or stocks of working materials; since the delay caused by the shortage of parts to go into larger assemblies is a major problem of manufacturing industry it is most important that every manager involved in storing or drawing supplies should understand the basic principles of inventory control. Nothing has a more devastating effect upon factory morale than continual interruptions to work caused by lack of material; nothing exasperates the customer more than the too frequent discovery that the shopkeeper is out of stock.

It is also desirable that, in addition to a knowledge of the commonest types of decision that arise in productive systems, the engineer should study the logical structure of a decision itself. Our analysis of strategies open to the manager may still be in its infancy, but the concept of balancing one's possible actions against the various states of nature, as the real situations of life are called, so as to choose that line which promises the greatest return for one's trouble—or the smallest loss, if gain is out of the question—is valuable. There are logical relations between the cost of the possible actions open to the manager, the likelihoods of these actions producing certain possible results, the reliability of the information on which he works and the scales of gain or loss involved in matching particular actions against particular states of nature. If one grasps this logical structure one then knows the information needed to select the proper strategy; and any advice to managers as to the nature of the right information they should assemble to do their work more effectively is advice worth having. It may even be that the improvement of the information services used by managers offers the quickest possibility of economic gain open to Britain as a nation. Decision theory should be part of any system of technical education; it may give the technologist little about dipping metals into liquids, but it may guide him as to the best number to dip in such and such a liquid at any given time. There may be some virtue in beginning this with students of twenty years of age or so; they should still be young enough to believe that a good decision can be taken at a level less personal than of intuition alone. Since the study of decision-strategy must necessarily entail the study of risk, it is also essential that the student acquires a working knowledge of elementary statistics with its concepts of significance, discrimination, concordance and so forth.

Conclusion

Technical education, if it enlightens at all, illuminates only a small part of the mind of the man who is to take responsibility for the affairs of industry. It undoubtedly helps both the designer and the toolmaker, so long as they are concerned solely with mechanism. But as soon as he is confronted with human problems, that is, with the majority of industry's problems, technical instruction alone is of little use to a manager. Indeed, it may be an illiberalising danger. But he cannot be better equipped to deal with the conflicts and breakdowns and interruptions that bedevil him (even though they are all human problems at their most human) simply by receiving what is at present called "liberal education". His task is to understand better the total organisation or work system inside which his particular technological knowledge is called into play. In acquiring this understanding there is, perhaps, a little that formal study can do for him; the literature of operational research is filled with interesting accounts of the use of analytical methods, with which the technologist should be familiar, in the better understanding of industrial problems. Nor need he be shy of discussing the human problems of industry examined in the field of the psychologists. Some of their concepts, like that of parataxis, may be strange. In the Seventeenth Century the idea of religious toleration was strange; Archbishop Laud drove the Pilgrim Fathers to America over an argument about the position of the cross in the church. The idea of national sovereignty was strange; a Spanish king died and bequeathed his whole empire to a young man. And the notion of force or acceleration was also strange. So we must not be surprised if inspectors of technical instruction or professors of mechanical engineering, in the Twentieth Century, regard the study of psychology as strange. But eventually the time will come when it will no longer be strange for technologists to think about the human beings who work for them or even, indeed to think a little about themselves; they could hardly make human relations in some enterprises any worse by doing so. Perhaps those of us engaged in technical education will find this reassuring.

THE NATURE OF OPERATIONAL RESEARCH

I

The General and the Particular

There is in Alice in Wonderland a Cheshire cat that, seated in a tree, and putting on a wide grin, holds a conversation with the little heroine. It then vanishes, leaving behind it only the grin looking down on Alice from the branches. To the writer, who happens to live in Cheshire, the difficulty of this feat is no greater than that of those who set out to distil certain elements from the manager's task and teach them, not as applied arithmetic but *as management practice*, in as abstract a context as, say, the syllabus of Latin or algebra. But one can no more separate the practice of management from what live managers are doing from hour to hour and as the beings they are than one can study the properties of grins on the faces of Cheshire cats that no longer exist. What not a few management theorists need to learn is that the field of understanding cannot be grins in the abstract, but grins-on-faces-of-cats-in-trees-talking-to-Alice. There is a form of geometry that deals with the shapes of cats' faces, but it has no special interest in grins. At the same time, many practical managers need a parallel lesson. They may, in the terms of this parable, be the Cheshire cats, and cats, as the world knows, are highly individualistic creatures. But neither

143

managers, nor the trees they find themselves up, nor the grins they have on their faces when talking to innocent girls, are so different among themselves as utterly to defy analysis. Nobody minimises the need for intuitive judgement and for common sense as important personal attributes of the manager, but these fundamental qualities alone are no longer adequate to directing the affairs of a modern industrial enterprise. In helping the manager to order his essential task, whoever he may be and whatever he may be called upon to manage (and this essential task is to identify his problems, to take decisions about them and to put these decisions into effect), the operational research worker may also have his contribution. The need is that managers should recognise that O.R. is not interested in grins as such, but in grins-on-faces-of-managers; it is the study of the particular generality, of the live case, of the word made flesh. What realist yet ever thought of lovemaking as an abstraction, something transcending the existence of actual women whom one has a real chance of meeting sometime?

Conscious Behaviour

The general aim of business or industrial enterprise—including the activities of public corporations, local authorities and non-profit making trusts—does not essentially differ from the rational or intelligent ambitions of any individual person. This is to secure the best use (or profits) from whatever resources are available; in the final analysis this is part of a common desire to attain the greatest security in the conditions of existence as we experience them. All rational behaviour must, to some extent, anticipate the future. It is intended to bring about some conditions of affairs more acceptable than the condition that would have arisen had some other course of action (including to do nothing) open to the human subject been followed. On that account, it needs to answer the three following questions:

What is to be done?
What is the organisation for doing it?

How are its physical demands fulfilled?

This trinity of questions can be briefly suggested more specifically in particular fields; such as

military: strategy, tactics, weapons.

government: specification, supervision, processes.

manufacturing: specification, supervision, processes.

hospital: diagnosis, nursing, drugs.

building: architectural design, site organisation, craft operations.

The principal activity of managers, at all levels in the enterprise, is to ask these questions; the act of answering them is generally known as taking decisions. It is often said that the peculiar function of a manager is to take decisions, but such a definition must assume that the manager has first identified the decisions he needs to take. Different levels of managers deal with different types of questions rather than with others; for example, the Board are generally concerned with choice of policy; the management with the supervision of the total operations; the foremen and chargehands with the final physical processes. Decisions may be classified as follows:

choices from all available policies;

choices from all feasible management plans likely to fulfil chosen policy;

choices from all processes or tools to carry out chosen management plans.

Decisions are taken to overcome problems that lie in the path of achievement; in the fields of processes and tools the manager has very considerable assistance from the discoveries of science and technology.

Variety and Risk

Operational research is concerned to identify and analyse the problems that arise at the levels of strategy and tactics, or of policy and supervision, and, if possible, to suggest solutions to

11

those problems. It is thus much less specific than technology, since in discussing possible policies and systems of management it must have regard to activities not entering into technology proper; such activities may be economic, psychological and social. It is also much concerned with questions of uncertainty, both as random or disordered sequences of events, or as inexact or even deliberately misleading information; and, to an extent more than any technology, it needs to give close thought to the validity and interpretation of its findings. The number and importance of the variable quantities that enter into human or real life situations are such as to make results that are valid in one set of conditions more often than not inappropriate in others; in technology, on the other hand, although problems may be complex, the total field of interest is pervaded by certain general truths, such as the conservation of energy or the second law of thermodynamics. This frequently makes it relatively easy for the engineer who has solved one problem to see clearly and with confidence how his experience can be employed with success on a similar problem elsewhere, that is, systematically to learn.

The Search for Order

It is also a principal responsibility of the operational research worker to give logical form to the manager's main task. There is no simple definition of a management problem. All we can hope to do is to suggest some of the concepts that must be in front of the manager when he embarks upon the activity that seeks to recognise a problem and to frame a decision to deal with it. For decision-taking behaviour lasts only as long as there are problems to be dealt with, and rational beings avoid problems about which they are unable to do anything. Only mentally deranged persons contemplate taking action about impossibilities, such as reversing the direction of time, reviving the dead, establishing machines that produce perpetual motion, synthesising the elixir of life, and so forth; none of these would be regarded as fertile activities by professional managers.

II

The concepts of the "problem-decision" are of many kinds; while decision theory enables a logically tidy catalogue of them to be prepared the following paragraphs illustrate some of the immediate issues.

The Context

1. The relevance of the wider field inside which the "problem-decision" is generated.

Examples

(a) in deciding its military, naval or air defence strategy, a peacetime government should be clear about the ends for which any possible war may be fought; it is insufficient to define this merely as a desire to win;

(b) in deciding whether or not to enter a particular foreign market an enterprise should be aware of all other possibilities (including entering other foreign markets) that exist and that are, or may be made, available to it;

(c) before discussing how much extra warehouse accommodation a firm appears to need and where it should be located, the management should ask whether the amount of stock they plan to store in it could not profitably be reduced;

(d) in trying to save the time of hospital nurses, as, for example, by employing work study on the making of patients' beds, it is valuable to ask whether making of certain classes of beds could not be dispensed with altogether.

The First Summary

2. The immediate (or apparently immediate) essence of the problem itself; that is to say, a short definition of the unsatisfactory condition that must be changed. Although before the

change is finally achieved the apparent problem may have been transformed through several stages into quite a different one, it is always helpful to state in a few sentences what the problem is thought to be at the outset. This statement both concentrates attention and serves to communicate the ideas of one member of the management to another.

Examples

(*a*) at two otherwise comparable oil refineries, A and B, there appear, on average, to be more tankers waiting to take on or discharge cargo at B than at A; the immediate problem may be stated as "What action, if any, should be taken to reduce the waiting time per tanker at B to that at A?" (The possible fact, later to be discovered, that the cost of reducing the waiting time at B would be more than that of the time saved, and that B already has the lower discharge or loading cost overall, does not invalidate this precise postulation of the problem);

(*b*) in trying to improve the organisation of a hospital, it is essential to start with questions about the existing state of affairs, such as, "What do Matrons in fact do in the course of an average day (or week, or month)?", since it may be assumed that if organisation is bad, its effect upon a key person would be observable;

(*c*) at a factory (correctly regarded as exhibiting a high degree of management-worker co-operation) proposals for new wages rates, when a long-established hand process is mechanised, are rejected without discussion by the workers, to the astonished dismay of the management. The precise definition of the problem (as management believe it to be) is "What is it about the attitudes, motivations or other attributes of the workers that we either do not know, or have omitted to take into account?";

(*d*) a public transport corporation finds its costs in danger of exceeding its receipts; instead of asking general questions, such as, "What shall we do to save expenditure (or to increase revenue)?" it must state precise questions, such as, "We find the cost of receiving and checking the conductors' takings at the end of their turns to be of the order of £50,000 per year. Is this a reasonable figure? If not, what action do we take to reduce it?'"

The Value System

3. The scale, or scales, of values by which the problem is recognised, however imperfectly, to be a problem; problems imply the comparison of some desirable but imagined situation with some undesirable but existent situation, and the concept of desirability implies some scale or dimension of value or belief. It may very well be that the scales of value personal to different individuals called upon to handle the same problem are different. Such scales of value underlie the criteria of success or efficiency with which all management decisions are endowed, and, in taking decisions, it is important to recognise the reasons for adopting or accepting one mixture of values rather than another.

Examples

(a) a design problem may appear to be forced upon a manufacturing concern by published technical research which, if ignored by the concern, may give its competitors a significant market advantage; the solution to the problem will be judged by the design department, who may regard every new feature in the changed final product as a scientific victory, differently from the production department, who may regard every new feature as an organisational setback; the sales department may press for expensive changes irrespective of their cost and oppose any economies that they feel their customers may not like;

(b) a wages settlement highly satisfactory to the management may be regarded by the rank and file workers as capitulation on the part of their own union leaders; and prove, in the longer term, disastrous to the concern as a whole;

(c) a scheme of management apprenticeship may be regarded

by the chief accountant as a complete waste of precious current assets, but by other members of the management as vital to ensuring the continuity of the enterprise;

(d) in purchasing a machine or piece of plant it is possible to choose between alternatives in many different ways; one machine may be more expensive than others in upkeep and produce fewer products per hour in use, but its capital cost and its wages costs per hour may both be less.

The Exceptional Case

4. The need, if any, to give prominence to purely temporary or local factors, specific to the situation of difficulty, that in other situations would be overlooked or rejected, including the need to act expediently, or temporarily to set aside scales of value or criteria of efficiency on which emphasis would normally be put.

Examples

(a) to keep a promised delivery date for an important customer a manufacturer might consider taking certain components from a partially assembled job intended for another customer, despite his own frequently announced policy of "No Cannibalisation";

(b) a retail store might temporarily sell goods at a heavy loss in an attempt to capture the trade of a competitor;

(c) in taking disciplinary action against a particular employee for a flagrant breach of works' rules, a manager may find it expedient to depart from the accepted codes;

(d) in a period of rapid industrial change, or of economic crisis, a trading company may have to think about methods of advertising or terms of extending credit that it would, in other conditions, consider as improper.

The Nature of Information

5. The amount, nature, timeliness and accuracy of the information at the command of the management in identifying, dealing

with and subsequently ameliorating or eliminating the problem; and, in particular, the extent to which management is aware that its information may be inaccurate; and is, or may be, willing to regard the collection, processing or output of more accurate or timely information as relevant to the solution of the problem. (This is an element of problem identification and decision taking that is often rated as more important by outside observers than it is by members of the management directly concerned with the problem itself).

Examples

(a) a system of financial records, including internal audit, may supply a management with the unassailable assurance that the enterprise is honestly conducted at all levels and yet conceal an inevitable bankruptcy, since a majority of its transactions are not analysed so as to reveal that they in fact attract too low a margin of profit;

(b) the system of storekeeping records, however well designed to combat pilfering, may be of no help to management in establishing a logical stock control policy; in particular, daily or weekly variations of supply and demand, knowledge of which is essential for so doing, are not recorded except insofar as they contribute to periodic averages;

(c) the statutory returns demanded by the Minister of Power about accidents in coalmines, although elaborate and extensive, are not only of no use to colliery managers in in identifying the apparent causes of these accidents, but the very effort demanded in preparing them may exhaust any managerial interest in the more promising statistical analysis of a serious and urgent problem;

(d) a sample of hospital matrons may confidently assert that they are fully aware of the ward problems with which their overworked sisters are grappling; the same sisters, however, may produce evidence (convincing to an external observer) that their matrons are, on the contrary, largely out of touch with ward problems.

Apart from the functional inadequacies of particular channels of the information services normally available to management, it may at times be found that there is active obstruction to assembling the additional information needed for handling a particular problem; this is often the case when subordinate members of the management have reason to suspect that they may be held responsible for any trouble that may have been caused, but such obstruction may remain unknown to higher management.

Problem Prototypes

6. The underlying logical structure of the problem; this is, or may be, something quite different from its lucid definition in words or numerical terms, and is, in particular, the central theoretical interest of the student of management science or of operational research. As the problem becomes more closely defined by the very activity of trying to solve it, so may the manager's view of its logical structure be seen to change, and as more information is obtained about the problem, so its logical structure may be seen as increasingly complex. Some of the principal elements of problem-structures are given here; in practice, these elements, and others, may all be present in the same managerial task.

Examples

(a) communication problems; information needed for taking decisions must be, firstly, perceived or assembled; secondly, processed or interpreted; and thirdly, transmitted or re-issued. Not all of these steps may necessarily be taken by the same person, but, apart from questions of mutual intelligibility or goodwill, there are many sources of error in information systems. The study of these has become a subject in its own right, and it is inconceivable that the training of managers should continue to neglect it; the growth of methods of automatic data processing, particularly by electronic computers, is basically the rationalising of information systems;

(b) problems that are caused by demand temporarily exceeding supply; items may be requiring some kind of service at a rate that overtaxes the capacity of the agent providing it. This leads to the formation of queues, with items needing to wait for service; examples range from a string of diners lining up to pay for their meals to a national cabinet deferring business until its next meeting owing to lack of time;

(c) problems concerned with allocating limited resources, such as men or machines, to a number of different tasks, so as to fulfil as many of those tasks as possible with the least effort, or alternatively, to the greatest possible advantage; or to observe particular constraints, such as that certain men or certain machines can carry out only certain tasks at certain times; in its most complex form this type of problem is concerned with sequences of tasks carried out on the same article, such as a load of iron ore going through a blast furnace and a steel mill, and with fluctuations in volume of the work to be handled from one day to another;

(d) problems concerned with setting up fresh capital equipment, or with replacing existing plant or machinery, so as to secure, over the estimated life of the new capital asset, the greatest return; the problem thus demands a statement of how that greatest return is to be measured, that is, of what scale of values is to be chosen. Problems of this kind demand a knowledge of plant capacities, operating costs, maintenance costs, and estimates of the rates at which these change with age or use; they also raise interesting questions about the best ways to finance the new investment and the terms of the loans to be raised for doing so;

(e) problems concerned with the value of assets tied up in raw materials, work in progress and finished products.

These problems merge imperceptibly with those of technology, concerned with the speed of machines or methods of work, and with questions of finance, concerned with costs of raw materials and selling prices of finished products, but between these lies a wide range of complex problems concerned with two general needs (apart from others already mentioned in this section); they are

(1) the need to optimise the amount of material held at any point, or passing through any stage of the production unit, so that the total costs of holding it (involving deterioration, storage and insurance charges, rent, interest and so forth), of procuring a fresh batch of it (delivery, inspection or set-up charges) and of running out of it (delay, loss of goodwill or actual breakdown of defective plant), are minimised; and

(2) the need to optimise the quality of the material, so that, on the one hand, an excessive price or effort is not expended on having raw materials or finished goods too costly for their purpose, and, on the other hand, the raw materials, work in progress or final products are not falling short of the standards that, for the costs and prices aimed at, may be judged reasonable, either by maker or customer.

These problems are, in general, identified and controlled by three specific managerial techniques, namely, inventory control, cost control and quality control; it is comparatively rare, however, to find some unified or integrated system of regulating the total operations of a productive enterprise;

(f) problems concerned with subsequent actions following the outcome of decisions taken with incomplete knowledge of what those outcomes might be; in simpler terms —action A may be followed by any of consequences P, Q, R, etc. .... with varying degrees of probability; action

B may be followed by X, Y, Z, etc. . . . with varying degrees of probability; there is some choice between actions A and B, and a number of other actions, C, D, E, etc. each, in turn, with a train of consequences. Whatever action is chosen, there will be some consequence; a new set of conditions is thereby created, in which fresh action must be taken, giving rise to new conditions yet again; this process of interaction is repeated. But whatever decision is taken at the first stage limits the choice of decision at the second; the choice at the second, in turn, limits choice at the third and so forth. Since the model of this problem-decision is that of the game of draughts or chess, the study of it is known as game-theory and provides a strategy for detecting fraud; this theory is evidently of great theoretical interest to managers, but, in the absence of information, of restricted practical value;

(g) problems concerned with the behaviour of human beings in situations of authority and constraint; our knowledge of these is not yet sufficient to justify the claim that they may be understood theoretically, but there seem to be two main classes of problem:

    (i) those concerned with prestige or status among managers, often leading to the deliberate retention of operational facts of importance to competitors for favour or promotion;

    (ii) those concerned with motivation of workpeople, manifest by disputes over piece rates, incentive payment schemes, works rules and so forth;

As the human problems of different industries or of other enterprises, such as hospitals or universities, are investigated, so it becomes more clear that the underlying or logical structure of these problems is largely independent of the particular technology in which these human communities happen to be engaged;

(h) problems concerned with the viability of systems as such; just as electricity flowing round a network of conductors obeys certain laws of continuity about the input and output at points or junctions, so does the total activity or or values within an industrial network need to have regard to balancing certain flows; at the present moment our knowledge of systems analysis, or flows in networks, is hardly beyond the common-sense level, but the concept of the enterprise as a system of interacting flows is of great potential interest to managers.

III

The Possibilities of Action

The validity of a "problem-decision" depends in the final analysis upon effective action being taken to change the condition that had been recognised as unfavourable into the condition interpreted as favourable. Hence, any description of management activity is incomplete without some reference to the difficulties encountered in trying to implement decisions; the extent to which the difficulties are overcome and sufficiently clearly recognised to be remembered and dealt with in future problems is also, as the learning process, relevant to managerial behaviour. The claim of the operational research worker, or of the student of management science, is this: that despite the complexity, randomness and contradiction of the task of the manager, there exists a framework for treating many of his problems, and that this is sufficiently coherent to deserve a name of its own, a name given in order to identify its observational-analytical approach to preparing and effecting management decisions. This name is Operational Research; the techniques at its disposal may be drawn from all disciplines—from the attitude survey of the social anthropologist to the circuit theory of the electrical engineer. It is their unification into a scientific approach for the analysis of management problems that justifies the claim that such a subject exists, and, in particular, that it differs both from the intuitive approach of the born manager acting upon his hunches, and from the empirical approach of the practical manager steeped in his homely wisdom.*

The operational research worker recognises that, at all stages in the preparation of management decisions, and certainly in any attempts to put those decisions into practice, he is able only to forecast what is likely to happen. He does no more, and claims to do no more, than to estimate with less error than could be estimated, in any other way, what is likely to follow from such-and-such premises. In any given case he may be quite wrong, perhaps because the information was inadequate, perhaps because his grasp of the underlying logical structure of the situation was imperfect, perhaps because the methods adopted for analysing the situation were inadequate. But industry in general would probably be more economically administered if operational research were more widely employed, since this would mean the better use of whatever evidence were available in forming overall strategic aims, and in adopting or discarding particular tactics so as to fulfil these strategies. Such a trimming of the industrial or commercial course is itself perfectly consonant with the methods of science, which by continually subjecting its theory to the appeal of experiment, and by adopting, modifying or rejecting the theory in accordance with the observed results, provides a perpetual example of self-confident modesty in behaviour for the manager. For it is his task to suggest, not perhaps a scientific theory, but a plan of industrial action based upon the known facts, that may be tried out, or subjected to the test of experiment, not perhaps in the laboratory, but in the equally rigorous conditions of industry itself. The managerial process of control, of asking "Am I doing what I set out to do?" is exactly the counterpart of the scientist's question, "Do the

---

*"Look after your trade-union officials well, and they'll see there's no trouble with the men"; "Always tell a new salesman exactly what you want him to do and expect him to get on with it"; "I always judge a manager by the amount of paper I find on his desk"; "Never buy (or sell) copper (or cheese) on a rising (or falling) market"; "There's nothing like having a bit of healthy rivalry between the drawing office and the shop to keep everybody on their toes"; "Never have more than five (or six, or ten, or twenty) subordinates reporting to you", these are all secrets of practical managers communicated to the writer in moments of confidence.

predictions from my theory really come off when I experiment to test them?" And the scientist is trained—or should so be—to accept divergences between result and prediction as evidence of either incomplete knowledge or incorrect theory; in the the absence of experimental results he cannot know whether he should get more information or modify his theory, or both. To the manager with the scientific approach the results of experience should be no less instructive than for the scientist; the laboratory of industrial or commercial effort provides the evidence for accepting, modifying or rejecting the plans on which the manager is trying to act—and, above all, for seeing such acceptance, modification or rejection in a reasonably objective spirit.

IV

Future Developments

To assert that management, at least in Britain, is, at best, luke-warm about operational research and, at worst, openly hostile to it, would be to state a case to which the advertisements in the Sunday newspapers for operational research workers lend no support. The demand for experienced men far exceeds the supply. But the means of training new staff are inadequate, and the task of doing so is made harder than it need be by a delibe-rately contrived shortage of published material of interest to operational research workers in general; even in university seminars on the subject it is still often difficult to persuade industrial firms that their representatives should discuss freely any studies they may have undertaken. This is not solely because a majority of industrialists still believe that the universities are necessarily out of touch with practical affairs, although they will undoubtedly remain sceptical about the value of university opinion upon, say, investment or manpower policy, long after they have become accustomed to seek (and often to accept without question) university advice upon metallurgical or electronic affairs. It is because, in the management of British

industry at least, the use of scientific method is still new; intellectual effort is still frequently regarded as the activity of
back-room boys, blind-fold sprites to be carefully shielded from
the consequences of their mischievous tricks by the superior
judgement of their employers; the expert, as one half-truth puts
it, must be on tap but not on top. These attitudes are only partly
due to insecurity among top-management; there is not time to
keep pace with the latest developments in scientific method and
it is therefore as well not to engage too deeply in discussions
that involve not only new ideas but, inescapably, alas, a new
vocabulary. They are also due to the intensely personal character
of the management function; it is impossible to discuss a management problem in the abstract, as an exercise in adjusting
destiny, remote from the person who must carry out the adjustment. It is no easier to understand an act of management without also understanding the personal values and character of the
manager than it is to see a smile on the face of our disappearing
Cheshire cat; the personality of the manager, placed somewhere
along a spectrum that ranges from delusions of grandeur to
congenital vacillation, but closely grouped as to the vast
majority around a norm of intelligent scepticism, is, to the
operational research worker, a fact, and a highly significant
fact, of the total situation with which he is called upon to deal.
To him, the catalogue of misunderstanding that may be assembled to describe the conception that many managers hold of
operational research is no less real; as, for example, that it takes
so long to find out anything of use as to be worthless in real life;
or that it is concerned only to turn the simplest facts into
elaborate mathematics; or that, on the contrary, it is nothing
new and can hence be safely ignored or disparaged; or that it
depends upon electronic computers costing hundreds of thousands of pounds; such mythology is as much the material of his
task as bank rate, the capacity of the foundry, the number of
lorries available or whatever may be the operational facts of the
problems that management may refer to him. But this catalogue
of misunderstanding is, in turn, a perfectly natural phase in the
history of management; just as most manufacturers seventy

years ago derided the idea of a drawing office, and just as many of them still regard systems of standard costing or quality control today as useless extravagances (and operational research can often prove such managers to be right), so must its own acceptance prove to be both partial and reluctant. However this may be, time is always on the side of the sciences, and we are at the moment watching the birth of a new one: the study of practical achievement through improved decision-making. An Operational Research it was good enough to help us win a World War; the danger, and it is one that managers alone can avert, is that, deprived of the chance to help practical men handle their practical difficulties, it will become precisely what, by some senior managers, it is already seen as being—an expensive source of insults from inexperienced men of half one's age.